WHAT DID YOU SAY STOPPED PLAY?

25 YEARS OF THE
WISDEN CHRONICLE

WISDEN

EDITED BY

Matthew Engel

ILLUSTRATED BY

Nick Newman

WISDEN
Bloomsbury Publishing Plc
50 Bedford Square, London, WC1B 3DP, UK

WISDEN and the wood-engraving device are trademarks of
Bloomsbury Publishing Plc

First published in Great Britain 2018

www.wisdenalmanack.com
www.wisdenrecords.com
Follow Wisden on Twitter @WisdenAlmanack
and on Facebook at Wisden Sports

A catalogue record for this book is available from the British Library

Library of Congress Cataloguing-in-Publication data has been applied for

ISBN: HB: 978-1-4729-5438-1; eBook: 978-1-4729-5439-8

2 4 6 8 10 9 7 5 3 1

Typeset in Haarlemmer MT by Deanta Global Publishing Services, Chennai, India
Printed and bound by CPI Group (UK) Ltd, Croydon, CR0 4YY

To find out more about our authors and books visit www.wisdenalmanack.com
and sign up for our newsletters

CONTENTS

INTRODUCTION

Just after the turn of the millennium I gave up my post as editor of *Wisden Cricketers' Almanack* and went with my wife and children to live in America. In July 2003 I came back to do a second stint as editor. And the very first weekend after our return we went to Hampshire for a family celebration.

The weather was a deceitful welcome-home present from heaven: it was gorgeous. And from the window of our hotel bedroom, against a lovely wooded backdrop, it was possible to see a cricket match going on. Brockenhurst v Ellingham. It might have been part of the same gift. Naturally I wandered down to have a look.

I had been there only a few minutes when suddenly there was a rustling in the woods, followed by the appearance of a herd of New Forest ponies who galloped on to the outfield and settled somewhere around deep extra cover before being shooed away.

It was enchanting in all kinds of ways, not least aesthetically. But it also seemed like the final part of the gift. While in America, I had bonded with cricket's long-lost cousin, baseball. Nothing much seems to stop baseball except a hurricane or a mass punch-up. Cricket, though, is much more fragile, especially in England where hot, dry summer days can never be taken for granted.

Also, the ball is supposed to bounce en route to the bat, which means the surface is far more important: if someone dug a hole ten feet in front of home plate, it wouldn't matter that much. And because cricket – proper cricket – goes on longer, the world impinges much more. We stop for lunch and tea; players can spend hours, even days, without actually having to appear on the field. It is part of life rather than a distraction from it.

And, for some reason I cannot wholly explain, cricket is just more, um, eccentric. What is it about the game? People do not habitually take footballs and baseballs to the North and South Poles; into slate mines; to the tops of mountains and the bottom of lakes; and on to rarely visible sandbanks miles from reliably dry land. They take cricket balls – and bats, stumps and bails. Perhaps it is some kind of reaction to the need for conditions to be just-so before a traditional match can begin.

When I was first appointed editor of *Wisden* in 1992, people who didn't know much about it would say something like "Oh, yes, that's the book that records all the strange things that happen in cricket." Well, it certainly recorded some of them, but not in any systematic way.

My predecessors were all sensible enough to have more important things to do. But I have always had a habit of flicking through newspapers, looking for something to catch the eye: and I had for three years co-edited a short-lived, more jokey kind of all-sports Wisden called the *Sportspages Almanac* (without the quaint K) which specialised in recording unusual events. Cricket was, naturally, the richest seam. So I wanted to import some of that jollity.

It was impossible to start at once: it was mid-year and there were more urgent priorities. But at the start of 1993, I brought out the scissors again and began filing any cuttings that referred to cricketing oddities, and thus the Chronicle started. Since then, the world has changed hugely, cricket and newspapers more than most things (not necessarily for the better). But the Chronicle has survived – triumphantly, I like to think – and this not-all-that-slim volume is a celebration of its first quarter-century: a selection of the couple of thousand items that have appeared in that time.

Not all the items are funny, as the Tragedy section illustrates all too vividly. Not all of them are weird: many record remarkable perform-ances – just one item that very first year was about a 15-year-old schoolboy from Lancashire who had scored an unbeaten 234 in 20 overs. His name was Andrew Flintoff.

Cricket has Laws but *Wisden* has rules. And to govern the Chronicle I instituted a new one: there had to be a source – it had to be reported elsewhere before *Wisden* would mention it. I was terrified of hoaxes.

Indeed, there were two of my friends I identified as potential perpetrators. But in cricket it is hardly necessary to make stuff up: the truth is often far stranger than the most imaginative fiction.

And in those days, there was a clear route for the strangeness to be reported. British local newspapers used to employ quaint figures known as "journalists". And on a summer Monday one of the youngsters might ring round his club-secretary contacts to ask them about the weekend matches. And one of them might start wittering about how Buggins had scored a fifty and that Scruggins had taken a few wickets.

And then, just once in a while, the official might perchance just mutter, half to himself: "Now, was that before or after the elephant stopped play...?" And the journalist would suddenly wake up and say "WHAT did you say stopped play?" "Oh, yes, didn't I mention the elephant?" And before nightfall, after a lot of scurrying round, the journalist would have flogged the story to all the nationals and be celebrating the impending windfall with pints all round.

To the best of my knowledge, no elephant has yet stopped play[1]. But pretty much everything else in the animal kingdom has. I'm just saying that's how news used to travel. Nowadays, the few remaining office-bound, screen-slave, time-poor local journalists might never find out about it. The compensation is that there are now club websites, Facebook pages, Twitter feeds and video cameras in everyone's pocket. So an elephant on the pitch should not escape notice.

The internet revolution was well established by the time I returned from the US, and it enabled the Chronicle to become more global, with many more stories coming in from countries where elephants are more likely to stop play. The big growth was in stories from the subcontinent, especially from India where cricket advanced from being merely a national game to something approaching a national religion. And, in

---

[1] One was paraded at lunchtime at The Oval in 1971. And, as this book records, one might yet appear during play at Hambantota, Sri Lanka.

contrast to more developed countries, the Indian news media were becoming more vibrant rather than less.

This was a mixed blessing for Chronicle, because a large percentage of the stories from South Asia tended to be brutal rather than barmy. This book is intended to reflect the weird things that happen in cricket. It is occasionally poignant, sad and sometimes horrifying. But it is primarily meant to be funny, and subcontinental stories often involved argumentative boys in back alleys bashing each other with bats with fatal consequences. I have included enough of these to give a flavour but I hope not enough to induce nausea.

It is not just in Asia that the game has become more disputatious. Cricket in England has become less ubiquitous but is taken much more seriously by those who continue to play it. Throughout the book, there is more unpleasantness after the millennium than before. The Chronicle reflects the game, and the world we live in.

On the other hand, there is also more of everything. The section has grown bigger with the passing years, and – I am confident of this – better. In the 2005 *Wisden* the section began to be adorned by Nick Newman's wonderful cartoons. (And Nick has produced another brilliant selection for this book to cover the missing years.) In 2012 it was moved to a new place of honour at the very back of the book, and all sports enthusiasts are used to reading the back page first.

I was editor of *Wisden* myself for almost half the Chronicle's first twenty-five years. I am very grateful to the other four editors of the era – Graeme Wright, Tim de Lisle, Scyld Berry and Lawrence Booth, the current incumbent – for supporting and nurturing the section on their watch. And to Hugh Chevallier, now co-editor, who has been the unflappable behind-the-scenes production mastermind for the past twenty editions, and to Christopher Lane, the consultant publisher, who has been crucial to the business side of *Wisden* for the past thirty. For reasons I don't understand, neither seems to have aged much.

Lawrence, Hugh and Chris have all made Chronicle-compiling much easier by being such skilful snappers-up of unconsidered trifles, as has another Wisden lifer, deputy editor Steven Lynch. So too Harriet

Monkhouse who, year after year, corrected mistakes that eluded everyone else. I am also grateful to my regular spotters from further afield: Prakash Dahatonde, Rajesh Kumar and Nirav Malavi in India; Mahendra Mapagunaratne who monitors Sri Lankan news; Mike Bechley and David Lamming are regular contributors from the UK. I miss the late Bob Harragan, a splendid character who until he died in 2016, too young, ensured that goings-on in south-west Wales were never under-represented. And I owe special thanks to Rob Steen, who compiled the section during my absence in America.

We always welcome contributions from readers, wherever they are. And weblinks or simple steers will be gratefully received at almanack@ wisdenalmanack.com.

All kinds of crazy cricketing life is in the Chronicle, but not everything crazy that now gets reported in *Wisden*. If something odd enough happens in a game that the Almanack would cover anyway it should get mentioned in the match report and, since 2000, listed even further back in the book in what is known in-house as "the odds" – the Index of Unusual Occurrences.

The Cricket Round the World section (established 1993) snaffles items from the game's more improbable outposts. These were anthologised in the 2014 collection, *Elk Stops Play*. Other snippets from different sections of *Wisden*, dating back to the Almanack's Victorian infancy, were collected in the 2007 book *Parachutist at Fine Leg*. So the "WHAT did you say stopped play?" section of this book cannot mention the elk or the parachutist. Nor:

Battle of Britain stopped play (Lord's, 1940)

bomb scare stopped play (Lord's, 1973)

baggage delayed on Indian roads (Rajkot, 1988)

groundstaff forgetting to mark fielding circles (Perth, 1989)

fried calamari (when Daryll Cullinan hit a six into a barbecuing spectator's frying pan and the ball had to cool down) (Paarl, 1995)

bungee jumping (Hove, 2000)

Gurkha pipe band (Canterbury, 2002)

gridlock in London (The Oval, 2002)

umpire taking pictures (The Oval, 2003)

arrival of Royal Mail ship (St Helena, 2004)

mortar attack (Baghdad, 2004)

ground not appearing on satnav and team getting lost (Rotterdam, 2005)

wedding (Ascension Island, date unknown)

plus the fact that "wild women" are always likely to stop play in Western Samoa. Unfortunately, "wild women" is the local term for cyclones.

But I've just mentioned them anyway.

Nor have I been able to include my own contribution to cricket history: umpiring what we believe to be the world's most southerly cricket match, less than a mile from the South Pole, in 2012 (temperature: minus 28°C). However, as a bonus, at the back of the book there is a selection of some of the Chronicle-style items that appeared in the *Sportspages Almanac*, covering 1989, 1990 and 1991. Thanks due here to my collaborator in those distant days, Ian Morrison, and to Simon Barnes, whose column in *The Times* was then a rich source of material.

One hitherto impossible Stopped Play has so far got away, infuriatingly. In the summer of 2017 *Test Match Special* mentioned a case of Drone Stopped Play, apparently somewhere in the Midlands. But the words vanished into the ether and, despite the best efforts of the *TMS* production team, it has not yet been possible to hunt down the precise story. There will be a repetition soon enough, no doubt.

I haven't included the New Forest ponies either: happens all the time in Brockenhurst, apparently. However, there is an item from nearby Lymington, where in 2017 they played a match against Bashley, bowling from only one end to thwart vandals who had dug up the pitch. The report in the *Bournemouth Daily Echo* began "Lymington and Bashley are unlikely to receive a mention in *Wisden*…"

They were wrong about that. And I hope *Wisden* will go on reporting the glorious and global eccentricities of our game forever.

This book is not really about cricket, it's about life.

MATTHEW ENGEL
Herefordshire, June 2018

NOTE TO READERS

The date given at the end of each paragraph in the text refers to the year the event happened or was originally reported. The item would have appeared in the following year's *Wisden*. The same applies to the dates in the Prequel section, for the items from the *Sportspages Almanac*.

AGELESS

1

AGELESS

Les Kempster, 70, took ten for 34 playing for a team put together by the former Sussex player John Denman against Worth Abbey School at Crawley. Kempster is a part-time cleaner at the school. (1993)

Ivor McIvor of Fochabers, Morayshire, who at 73 claims to be Britain's oldest village league cricketer, received a letter of congratulations from the Prime Minister after concluding his forty-eighth season. "I don't know if he's the oldest but he's certainly the most stupid. He's had nine operations for varicose veins and he still insists on playing," said his wife Rita. (1994)

Jack Swain, 73, collapsed and died seconds after bowling his final over in his retirement match at Cuckfield, Sussex. The match was abandoned but a planned farewell supper went ahead as a tribute to him. (1995)

David Church of the East Woodhay club, Newbury, completed forty years of club cricket without missing a match through injury. (1996) *Church eventually extended his sequence to forty-five years.*

Arthur Cuthbertson, a 70-year-old slow left-arm bowler from Caversham, Berkshire, took nine for 38 against Whitchurch, including a hat-trick, immediately after undergoing two eye operations. "At least I can see the stumps again," he said. (1997)

Keith Hookway, 60, from Bexhill, has played his 600th consecutive match for St John's in Sussex, having never missed a game since the club was founded twenty-two years ago. (1998)

Stan Rudder, at 63 believed to be the oldest player in the competition, hit the last ball of the match for four to give Waterlooville a one-wicket win over Hambledon in the National Club Championship. (1998)

Cyril Heath, 78, took eight for 44 at Ashburton, Devon. He said his trick was "always thinking I'm 39 next birthday". (1999)

Jack Hyams, 81, a retired pet-shop owner from Hertfordshire, lost his chance to become the oldest cricketer to appear at Lord's when the match between Cross Arrows and the Royal Household was rained off. (2000)

Ted Martin, the Western Australia leg-spinner who took six MCC wickets for his state during the 1932–33 Bodyline tour, has become the first Australian first-class cricketer to reach the age of 100. "It's nice to have beaten Bradman at something," he said. (2002)

Ray Mortimer, 70, took a hat-trick for Woodgreen against Ordnance Survey in the Hampshire League. Mortimer, a regular until 1998, now usually umpires but played his first league game of the season because the team was short. (2006)

The World's Oldest Eleven (average age 75.5) lost by one wicket to the World's Second-Oldest Eleven (all over 70) at Poplar Oval, Melbourne, during the annual interstate Over-60s carnival. Brendan Lyons, the 80-year-old son of former Australian prime minister Joseph Lyons, was the senior man on the field. "They all clank like medieval armour when they walk out," said Jim Murphy, 73, captain and most junior of the Oldest Eleven, "but they're all bloody legends at their own clubs." (2007)

Midsomer Norton spin bowler Jim Eyles, 72, took six for 40, the best figures of his life, against Avonside. His son Craig took three of the other wickets. (2011)

Jim Smallbone, 63, took two successive five-wicket hauls for Hampshire Over-60s a year after collapsing on the field, when his heart stopped for

at least twenty minutes. He credited Mike Tindall, a first-aider who was keeping wicket for Sussex Over-60s, with keeping him alive until the air ambulance arrived. (2013)

Rupert Webb, the 91-year-old former Sussex wicketkeeper, confronted a motorist who attacked a traffic warden on the streets of Worthing. Webb saw a "well-built man" punch the warden and break his glasses. "I had a firm grip on my walking-stick and I was about to give the attacker a jolly good clout," said Webb. "Fortunately, at that moment, a police car came round the corner and the man was arrested and taken away." Webb is also known for his acting, especially his role in the film *Four Weddings and a Funeral*. Police said a 60-year-old man had been cautioned for assault. (2013)

The former West Indian all-rounder Collis King, 62, has scored his fiftieth century in twelve seasons with Dunnington of the York Senior League. (2013)

Eileen Ash of Norwich credited her Tuesday morning yoga sessions for keeping her fit at the age of 101. Mrs Ash, who played for the England women's team (as Eileen Whelan) before and after the Second World War, gave up golf for bowls aged 98. (2013) *See also 2017.*

Commentator Henry Blofeld is to marry for the third time, aged 74. "Valeria," he said delightedly, "is the only girl I've met who loves what I do." (2013)

An 80-year-old man, born with one hand, took five wickets in eight overs. Left-arm spinner Bill Robinson from Bradford was a late call-up into the Yorkshire Terriers team playing Shropshire in the National Disabled League. "I was determined to play at least one game," he said. "I think the team want me to play a lot more." (2014)

Renfrew Second Eleven's eighth-wicket pair put on only 15 against Uddingston Seconds, but their stand was notable for the spectacular age gap. David Barr (aged 83 years and 277 days) was batting with Muhaymen Majeed (11 years and 242 days). Both were called up because of a player shortage. The partnership was marked by Muhaymen's successful insistence that his partner should run quick twos. Renfrew, still one man short, lost by seven wickets. (2014) *See also 2017.*

Mick Massey, 82, took five for 38 for the Hatherleigh midweek team in Devon against the Englefield Green touring side. This increased his determination to continue for another season. His captain, David Manning, said: "I'm 68, but I can't even think of packing up when Mick's doing so well." (2015)

John Reynolds, 83, has announced his retirement after sixty-four years of club cricket in Norfolk due to "worn-out knees". He took 5,811 wickets, including 14 hat-tricks. (2017)

The 86-year-old actor Brian Jackson ("The Man from del Monte") and 12-year-old stand-in John Child were together at the crease at the end of

Stage Cricket Club's match against Maidenhead & Bray, a 74-year age gap. (2017)

Eileen Ash (née Whelan), the last survivor of the first women's Test played in England in 1937, marked her 106th birthday on October 30 by taking a flight in a Tiger Moth over the Norfolk coast. The plane was a mere 76-year-old. (2017)

2

ANIMAL MATTERS

Dave Cutting, 36, was bitten by an adder as he went out to bat at Hastings, Sussex. (1993)

More than sixty people offered to give a home to a stray mongrel who ran on to the pitch at Trent Bridge as Merv Hughes was about to deliver the first ball of the Third Test. Graham and Sally Bosnall from Derby, who adopted him, followed the example of the staff at the RSPCA shelter and called him Merv. (1993)

Wally Lloyd, a spectator at a match between Kington and a Herefordshire Select Eleven, caught an escaped pet kestrel on the outfield by tempting it with a piece of ham. (1994)

Blair Sellers, playing for South Melbourne in the Dowling Shield Under-16 competition, hit a lofted drive that was stopped by the back of a seagull's head, turning a certain four into two. He was not unduly upset by this until he was bowled for 98. The seagull recovered. (1995)

Bruce, a ten-year-old Labrador with a talent for sniffing out lost cricket balls, discovered his 500th ball in a cemetery at Sacriston, County Durham. His 88-year-old owner, Jack Moralee of Chester-le-Street, regularly gets calls from clubs asking for Bruce to comb fields near their grounds. (1995)

Purdey, a golden retriever, has been made vice-president of Hutton Cranswick Cricket Club in Yorkshire after finding fifty lost balls. (1996)

Bodie, a Jack Russell terrier, found his 500th lost ball for the club at Shanklin, Isle of Wight. (1997)

Players at the annual Reedybrook Ashes, in the Queensland outback, killed several pythons and one deadly taipan snake while looking for lost balls. (1998)

The treasurer of Builth Wells Cricket Club in Wales, sent out to buy a strimmer to keep the ground under control, bought two goats for £20 to do the job instead. (1998)

Paul McIntosh, a cricket-mad 11-year-old from Northampton, named his new pet rabbit Hansie, after the South African captain, Hansie Cronje, three days before Cronje's downfall for his role in the match-fixing scandal. "We couldn't believe it," said Paul's mother, Elaine. "Our nine-year-old, Lauren, has been telling everybody that our rabbit has been arrested." (2000)

A Pomeranian dog called Fred became a member of Chorley Cricket Club, in Lancashire. His owners, Beryl and George Ritchie, paid the £25 subscription so Fred could go into the bar for his regular helping of beer. (2000)

A black Labrador has had a trophy named after him – the Sam Challenge Trophy – by Bridgend Cricket Club in South Wales. Sam has saved the club hundreds of pounds by finding lost balls in the undergrowth, with a record twenty-seven in one season. "If some of our fielders could get to the ball as well as Sam, we would be league champions," said club chairman Jake Collier. (2000)

After winter floods, pre-season preparations at Trent Bridge were further disrupted by frogs. Groundsman Steve Birks, hitherto distracted by ducks swimming on the square, discovered the frogs jumping out of water machines; he insisted his groundstaff put them into buckets and march them down to the Trent. "A bit slimy," he said, "but, then again, so are some of our players." (2001) *The headline in the* Nottingham Evening Post *read: "I've toad you… now hoppit"*.

Usman Tariq hit six sixes in an over for Whitefield against Tranmere Victoria in the Merseyside Competition but progress was slow. A dog in an adjacent park intercepted the first blow and returned the ball only after a lengthy debate; it was less forgiving two deliveries later, allowing a fielder to retrieve the ball, then biting him. (2001)

Four Labradors have been trained to hunt for lost balls in the thick gorse surrounding the ground at Scot Hay, Staffordshire. The dogs have found every one: 120 this season alone. "The dogs are on their feet as soon as they hear the thwack of bat on ball," said one of the owners, former Staffordshire bowler Ben Griffiths. "We just shout 'Fetch'." (2001)

Villagers in Lynton, north Devon, called for a cull of more than fifty goats in the Valley of Rocks after the herd fouled local amenities, including the pitch at one of England's most picturesque cricket grounds. The breed is said to date back six thousand years and is mentioned in the Domesday Book. Opponents condemned the proposal as "cruel and unnecessary" and suggested erecting a goat-proof fence. (2003) *A cull was still on the agenda in 2014 when the goats were munching on local gardens.*

Australians should use their cricket bats to whack cane toads, the imported pest that is threatening to overrun Queensland, said Liberal MP David Tollner. The RSPCA called the advice inhumane. (2005)

British scientists took rubber from a cricket-bat handle to help save the koala, whose population has declined from millions to less than 100,000. The rubber was used to line a tube that collected sperm from male koalas for an artificial insemination programme designed to guard against inbreeding. (2006)

A horse pulling a cart full of building material was killed after being hit on the head by a cricket ball while passing a cricket ground near Chandigarh. Owner Paramjeet Singh said his livelihood was ruined. Eyewitnesses said the horse was in terrible pain for twenty minutes before dying, and that the cricketers did not apologise. (2007)

The pads on the feet of tree frogs have shown scientists in India how to make a sticky coating which, they say, could help them make fumble-free gloves for wicketkeepers. (2007)

Hampshire are to ban dogs from the Rose Bowl because they found insurance companies unwilling to cover clubs for the risk of injury, although they were willing to insure against terrorist attack. (2008)

A two-year-old pied cock pigeon called "Tubby" (named after Mark Taylor) beat eleven other contenders also named after cricket commentators in the inaugural Great Betfair Pink Pigeon Race over a thirty-kilometre course from the Glenn McGrath Oval in Narromine to Trangie. The event was held to raise money for the McGrath Foundation, in honour of Glenn's late wife Jane. "Tubby" finished just ahead of "Scoop" (Simon O'Donnell) and "Warnie". (2009)

Residents living near the County Ground at Hove called police after hearing gunshots after midnight. Sussex County Cricket Club later admitted that they had brought in a pest-control company to shoot a fox.

Chief executive Dave Brooks said it had been causing problems by "scratching around on covers and acting oddly". He insisted: "We really didn't want to do it, but it was a last resort." (2010)

An animal-rights group has lodged a legal complaint against the Indian Test player-turned-politician Navjot Sidhu after he arrived at a court hearing on an elephant. (2012)

The former Zimbabwean cricketer Guy Whittall spent a peaceful night while an eight-foot crocodile was hiding under his bed. It is thought to have sneaked into his room the previous night at the game lodge where Whittall is a director. He was unaware of his bedfellow until he went to the kitchen for breakfast and heard the maid scream. "The really disconcerting thing is the fact that I was sitting on the edge of the bed that morning, barefoot and just centimetres away from the croc," he said. (2013)

Shane Warne was bitten on the face by a juvenile anaconda while competing in *I'm a Celebrity… Get Me Out of Here!* "It's non-venomous but very aggressive," said a Network Ten spokesperson. "Anacondas have a hundred rear-facing teeth. Being bitten by one is like getting a hundred hypodermic needles at once." (2016)

Yorkshire coach Jason Gillespie, who became vegan two years ago, said he regretted that the Wensleydale Creamery sponsored the club. "Yes, they are a sponsor," he said. "But it doesn't mean I agree with what they do. It's out of my control, just like the fact that cricket balls are made of leather." He added: "Hopefully one day the dairy industry can be shut down. I think it's disgusting and wrong on so many levels." (2016)

An 18-year-old fast bowler from Croston, Lancashire, spent several days on an IV drip after being bitten by a red-bellied black snake in a club match in Sydney. Joe Lyth, fielding on the boundary for Pennant Hills, had to collect a six hit into nearby undergrowth when he disturbed the snake, which then nipped him on the heel. He told his family at home he had been injured rather than bitten, calculating that it would worry them less. (2017)

Game wardens have been deployed in Sri Lanka to stop wild elephants straying onto the pitch during the three one-day internationals against Zimbabwe at Hambantota. The stadium is next to an elephant sanctuary, and close to a patch of jungle. Elephants have occasionally invaded the pitch at night, but not during a match. (2017)

Parkhead Cricket Club, in Sheffield, is considering using human urine on the outfield to help deter badgers who have been tearing up the turf. (2017)

3

APPLIANCE OF SCIENCE

After researching the careers of 10,000 first-class cricketers, John Aggleton, a psychologist at the University of Durham, said that left-arm bowlers were likely to die two years earlier than right-armers. The former England left-arm spinner Phil Edmonds described the news as "depressing"... (1993)

... Researchers at the University of Durham have now concluded that left-handed bowlers are not necessarily likely to die younger than right-handers. However, left-handed bowlers have proved more likely to die in warfare; this may be because equipment and training are designed for right-handers. (1994)

Alan Clark, a maths student at the University of Hertfordshire, calculated that a throw returned on the bounce reached the wicketkeeper 0.05 of a second quicker than one returned on the full. (1995)

The Royal Economic Society newsletter called for the eradication of cricket after a paper by Howard J. Wall of Birkbeck College claimed that baseball-playing countries had growth rates substantially higher than those in cricketing countries. "We are not yet convinced," a Treasury spokesman said. (1995)

The British Psychological Society was told that fielders could quadruple their success rate at catching by practising under ultra-violet light. Dr Simon Bennett of Manchester Metropolitan University said it cut out distractions and enabled people to concentrate. (1998)

Cricket is as dangerous as skiing, according to research by David Ball of Middlesex University. For every 100,000 participants, 130 cricketers require hospital treatment in Britain every year. This makes the game the third most risky, behind only rugby and soccer, and equal with hockey and skiing. However, there were only two recorded fatalities among cricketers between 1988 and 1992. (1998)

A psychologist who studied thirty-three county cricketers found that they played better when they were feeling cheerful. Peter Totterdell of the University of Sheffield said there was a difference in performance of between six and 16%. (1998)

The introduction of neutral umpires has made no difference to the fairness of lbw decisions, according to statistician Dr Trevor Ringrose of Cranfield University. After looking at Test matches since 1977, Dr Ringrose concluded that there had been no difference in the application of the law since the international panel was established. However, he said that visiting batsmen in the Asian countries and Australia were more likely to be lbw than their opponents. (1999)

Sports scientists at John Moores University, Liverpool, endorsed Sir Donald Bradman's batting technique after subjecting it to "three-dimensional motion analysis". Professor Adrian Lees said their findings refuted suggestions that Bradman's wide, looping backlift made him a poor role model for young players. He said Bradman's unorthodoxy was "no worse" than the approved method. (2000)

Harry Barnes, a Manchester-based inventor, claimed to have solved the problems of contentious run-outs and stumpings in big matches after patenting a device called "Creasewatch". This involves using special electrical contacts between the stumps and bails. As soon as the bails are dislodged, video cameras would pick up the signal, removing the need for a third umpire to make a visual judgment. (2000)

Good batsmen take their eye off the ball to play fast bowling, according to researchers who studied three players wearing head-mounted cameras. The study showed that, after looking steadfastly at the ball as it left a bowling machine, they glanced at the spot where they expected it to bounce before fixing on the ball again. (2000)

Scientists believe missile-tracking technology could be used to remove the controversy from the lbw law. Researchers at Siemens are hoping to develop the Hawk-Eye system, which predicts trajectories, to calculate whether a ball would have hit the stumps. Sunset + Vine, Channel 4's cricket producers, said they were interested; the England and Wales Cricket Board said they were not. (2000)

Lester Allison, 35, a South African PE teacher, sought sponsors to enable full-scale production of a cricket box fitted with coil springs which, he claimed, significantly lessened the customary pain felt on impact. He tested its effectiveness by repeatedly hitting himself in the groin with a bat. Then, dressed only in a jockstrap, he subsequently invited onlookers to bowl directly at the target, only to retire hurt a few minutes later. (2001) *See also 2006.*

Inspired by Donald Bradman's famous childhood regime, an old-fashioned water-tank stand is being built at the New South Wales state training centre. Like the Don, youngsters will throw a golf ball against the brick base then attempt to hit the rebound with a stump. "Research identifies high-repetition skills as being key," said the high performance manager of NSW Cricket, Alan Campbell, "along with a strongly competitive but unstructured framework – backyard cricket, if you like." (2003)

Research at the University of New South Wales School of Optometry suggested short-sightedness might not be a disadvantage while batting. David Mann used a bowling machine to fire balls at batsmen wearing contact lenses that blurred their vision, and found they performed as well as they normally did. He speculated that short-sightedness may compel batsmen to play strokes later or concentrate harder to compensate for poorer vision. (2004)

Wearing a helmet may seriously affect quick thinking at the crease, according to a research paper presented to the British Psychological Society. Co-author Dr Mick Neave of Northumbria University said: "When your head gets too hot, the higher cognitive functions such as accuracy, response time and vigilance, are the first things to go." (2004)

Research by zoologists at St Joseph's College, Bangalore, showed that many professional cricketers exhibit the same fingerprint patterns. Almost all those they surveyed had the "ulnar loop" pattern on the right little finger. Their study was hindered because many Indian players refused to co-operate. (2004)

Jim Foat, the Gloucestershire batsman of the 1970s, has had an aspect of cellular metabolism named after him by a biochemist who happens to be a fan. In a paper in the journal *Progress in Lipid Research*, Simon Eavis of the Institute of Child Health in London coined the phrase "the Fat Oxidation Activity Transfer complex" (FOAT). Eavis said there was an unspoken challenge between him and a friend. Previously, Foat was most famous for brilliantly running out Tony Greig in the 1973 Gillette Cup final. (2005)

A man working at the Eden Project in Cornwall, who invented what was claimed to be the world's first eco-friendly cricket box, was hit while testing it out – in the face. Inventor Ben Foster suffered a cut eyebrow while facing Nottinghamshire fast bowler Charlie Shreck. His invention used hemp and a plant-based resin to be fully biodegradable. "The box stood up well," Foster said. "We just need to make an eco-friendly helmet." (2006)

The more Tests a cricketer plays, the longer he is likely to live, according to research conducted by the University of St Andrews. Using the data in *Wisden 2005* for players born before 1941, a team led by Professor Paul Boyle found that men who played more than twenty-five times for England lived four to five years longer than those who played twenty-five Tests or fewer. "If you are successful, you suffer less stress and feel positive about yourself, which appears to have a beneficial effect," Professor Boyle said. (2008)

Researchers from Loughborough University found that the behaviour of disruptive children improved after being introduced to cricket, even if it was only for a few hours. The study also found that cricket helped girls overcome "restrictive gender beliefs". One 11-year-old girl told researchers that she would get kicked if she played football with boys but added: "With cricket no one really tries to trick you and cheat. And we clap when someone does well." (2009)

The theory that moisture makes a cricket ball swing is false, according to researchers at Sheffield Hallam and Auckland Universities. Tests using 3D laser scanners and an atmospheric chamber, reported in the journal *Procedia Engineering*, found no link between humidity levels and sideways movement. Altitude and the age of the ball did have an effect, however. (2012)

Scientists trying to discover if there is intelligent life in space are planning to use the Laws of Cricket to test the aliens' ability to grasp difficult concepts. Members of the California-based SETI Institute (Search for Extra-Terrestrial Intelligence) want to use "Active Seti" – beaming material from the internet into the cosmos in the hope of a response – instead of just listening. SETI's senior astronomer Seth Shostak said: "If they look up cricket, there are descriptions, pictures, diagrams showing a pitch, and footage. They'll cross-correlate all this and put it together, and if they are clever at all, they will figure out something about cricket. Do they want to hear what the structure of the hydrogen atom is? No, they know that." (2015)

Researchers from the Australian National University in Canberra are studying what makes English willow the best bat-making material, in the hope of developing a cheaper alternative. Mohammad Saadatfar, from the university's school of physics and engineering, said the best bats were made from the female of one particular species of English willow. "It's too expensive, and it's just one small part of the world that is producing it," he said. "You want to diversify: the price is going up every year because it's just so limited, and there's no reason why every kid in the world should not play with a top-quality cricket bat." (2015)

Scientists have found that batsmen who bat "the wrong way round" have an advantage over players who use traditional methods. Professor Peter Allen of Anglia Ruskin University said that instinctively right-handed or left-handed players who learn to face the bowling the other way, with their dominant hand at the top, have technical and visual advantages. Professor Allen said the same effect may be true in both golf and baseball. (2016)

Chris Lintott, presenter of the astronomy programme *The Sky at Night* and a guest on *Test Match Special*, told Jonathan Agnew that working out how a cricket ball behaves was more complicated than understanding the workings of the universe as a whole. (2017)

... AND MAGIC

The mother of former Indian captain Sourav Ganguly hired a tantric (practitioner of black magic) to perform a special ceremony to ensure Ganguly's return to the national team, according to the priest. Kartik Chatterjee went from Kolkata to Lucknow to conduct the ceremony and announced that Ganguly would play for India again between July 15 and October 15. (2006) *He actually came back on December 15.*

The newly elected chief of Sri Lanka Cricket, Upali Dharmadasa, said he had held a *puja* – a Hindu prayer ritual – to drive out demons he held responsible for the board's cash crisis and the team's poor results: "I am a businessman and I know the effects of these evil spirits."(2012)

The owner of Chennai Super Kings passed his astrologer's advice on match strategy to the team's captain, Mahendra Singh Dhoni, during the 2013 IPL. The astrologer, Dr Venkatesan Karthikeyan, advised on toss and batting order, and suggested deities who should be propitiated before games. The ICC's anti-corruption unit and the police are aware of the emails. The team lost the final to Mumbai Indians. (2013)

... AND MAYBE SOMETHING IN BETWEEN

Former England opener John Edrich, 75, said he was cured of cancer by injections of mistletoe extract recommended by Stefan Geider, a doctor near his home in Aberdeenshire. Edrich was diagnosed with a rare blood cancer in 2000, and five years later appeared close to death. Seven years after that, he was back playing golf three times a week and saying he felt on top of the world. The plant has been known for decades to have some anti-cancer properties, but researchers say it can have terrible side-effects, and even Dr Geider admits: "It does not work for everybody. It's not a miracle cure." (2012)

AT LORD'S

The Marylebone Cricket Club received a letter addressed to a Mr O. F. Time, who had been selected to be one of the first to receive a brochure "full of beautiful items for home or boardroom". Stephen Green, curator of the Lord's museum, presumed that the letter was intended for Old Father Time, who he regretted was unable to enter into any correspondence. (1998)

MCC issued new dress instructions to cope with the presence of women in the pavilion, following the decision to admit them in 1998. Ladies were instructed to wear "dresses, skirts or tailored trousers" and cover their shoulders. Leggings were to be specifically barred. (1999)

MCC says it has been rejecting "regular" requests from docu-soap producers anxious to do fly-on-the-wall reports of the club's deliberations, especially over the admission of women. "I'm totally adamant that we would not want to open the club to that sort of exposure. Not yet," said head of marketing Chris Rea. (1999)

A tour of England by the Homies and Popz, a team of street kids from the tough Compton area of Los Angeles, was launched at Lord's. Many of the players, mostly Hispanic teenagers, were involved in gangs before they discovered cricket, "It's more exciting than baseball," said bowler Steve Aranda, "more of a man's game." "Cricket teaches you life," said coach Ted Hayes. "You play hard but you obey the rules." They later presented the Sinn Fein leader, Gerry Adams, with a hat. (1999)

Part of Lord's was sold for £2 million by Railtrack to an anonymous buyer, who is entitled to charge MCC rent for the next 137 years. The club's tenancy is protected. The land, about 800 square yards of the Nursery near the North Gate, is above the rail tunnel built in the 1890s leading to Marylebone Station. (1999) *After nineteen years of cold war mixed with intermittent collaboration, the buyer (property developer Charles Rifkind) and the club had still failed to reach an amicable solution by 2018.*

MCC has been selling an "official Lord's ball" stamped "made in England", which turned out to be almost entirely made in Pakistan. (2000)

MCC president Ted Dexter complained that reports of the Lord's turf being sold at £10 per square foot were erroneous. "We were extremely careful not to become metric martyrs," he explained, "so we complied with the written wishes of Westminster Council, and sold our turf in metric, rather than imperial measurements." (2002)

The *News of the World* launched a furious attack on the England and Wales Cricket Board after it wrecked an exclusive interview with England captain Michael Vaughan by emailing an advance copy of the text to two rival papers. Cricket correspondent David Norrie had sent the board a copy of the interview as a courtesy. Norrie said: "It's outrageous. After being immersed in the totally profes-sional world of the England rugby set-up for the past few months, I'd happily forgotten the antics of the Carry on Cricket bunch at Lord's." (2004)

Ten years after the MCC ended its men-only rule, only 62 women have become members, 0.3% of the total. (2008)

Scientists searching for possible new perfumes at Procter & Gamble have distilled the essence of Lord's. They have captured the odours of freshly cut grass, bats, laundered kit and the dressing-rooms (minus the players). "Perfumers need inspiration," said spokesman Will Andrews, "and this can come from people that surround them, places they've visited, or things that they love in the world." (2009)

Neil Nicholson and Kelli Fish became the first couple to book the Lord's pavilion for their wedding after MCC were granted a licence to hold marriage ceremonies. "Neil is a huge cricket fan," said Miss Fish. "I'd have been happy with getting married on a beach, but I'm really excited by this because he is excited." (2011)

MCC members expressed outrage at plans to organise a men's fashion event in the Lord's Pavilion, featuring a hundred male models. Although it was described as Savile Row-themed, one model said some outfits would be "relatively wacky". "Cricket has gone to the dogs," grumbled member George Burrough. "Every respected man who has played here will be looking on bewildered." An MCC spokesman said: "It's not something you could have done a decade ago; this is new. We are only just taking events to the next level." (2013)

MCC's ticket service began offering fifty-two possible titles for people to use when applying in the public ballot. These range alphabetically from Baron to Wing Commander, and also include Begum, Brother, Count, Don, Monsieur, Sheikh and, most improbably, Queen. However, the Royal Opera House boasts 129 options, including Viscondessa. MCC later reverted to six, excluding even Sir. (2015)

7

BANNED AND CAN'T PLAY ON

The former Pakistan international Parvez Mir was banned by the Carrow club in Norfolk for taking his mobile phone from the umpire and answering a call from his fiancée while he was bowling against Downham Market. (1995)

Wayne Radcliffe was banned for five years by the Wakefield & District Cricket Union for urinating on the pitch while fielding in the covers for Newmillerdam. He explained: "By the time a wicket fell I was desperate. I turned towards some trees and answered the call of nature. Hardly anyone saw." (1995)

Richard Stemp, the Nottinghamshire spin bowler, was suspended for the second time in a season while playing league cricket for Kimberley. He was banned for three matches for sledging a 15-year-old batsman, then banned for another four after being reported for dissent on his comeback against Radcliffe-on-Trent. (2000)

A village cricketer in Pembrokeshire has been banned for twenty-five years by the county association for leading an obscene chant against two rival players. Willie Morris, 39, barracked the Lamphey openers, both Australians, while watching a cup final against Hook. His team, Llangwm, had been knocked out in an earlier round. "I must be the first cricketer to be banned for twenty-five years simply for speaking his mind," said Morris. However, he admitted that he had earlier been banned from cup finals for five years. "The man is a habitual trouble-maker," said John Green, the Lamphey secretary. Brian James, secretary of Llangwm, said: "Lamphey's policy on importing cricketers is not popular." (2000)

A Perth club cricketer has been suspended for two matches for racist vilification. Bowler Peter Gardiner of Joondalup was having a staring match with a Gosnells batsman, Kyle Coetzer, when he said: "What are you effing looking at, you Pommy git?" Coetzer said he was not offended, and was Scottish, not English, anyway. But the umpire insisted on reporting the incident. (2005)

Four players were banned by the Quaid-e-Azam League in Yorkshire for terms ranging from three years to life after an attack on a teenage umpire. Fielders from the Bradford-based Shimla club hit 18-year-old Matt Lowson with the stumps after a series of decisions they disliked. (2009)

An 81-year-old great-grandmother, Margaret Burn, was suspended by Marsden Cricket Club in South Shields, the club she has supported for more than sixty years, after allegations of "suspected threatening behaviour towards junior members". Mrs Burn, who served the teas for many years, agreed she had told children to get off the pitch during a match, but denied swearing at them. "We have to follow protocol," said a club spokesman. (2013)

Five women cricketers from Multan were banned for six months by the Pakistan Cricket Board after they had alleged on a TV show that two male officials had demanded sexual favours in return for selection. A committee of inquiry said that three of the women had denied the original allegations, and the other two refused to present their case. (2013)

South Australia fast bowler Daniel Worrall was banned for two matches after scratching an image of a penis and testicles into a wicket being prepared for a grade final at Toorak Park in Melbourne. (2014)

Old Bournemouthians' opening batsmen got into a fight with each other after a dispute over a run in a Hampshire League game. Malick Kudmany and Peter Kritzinger received multiple match bans after Kudmany used racist abuse, and Kritzinger hit him in response. (2015)

Four students were suspended for five weeks from Rajarata University in Sri Lanka for playing cricket in front of the main administrative building during college hours. They were said to have interfered with university administration and damaged vehicles and flowers. (2016)

Former England fast bowler Steve Harmison was given a twelve-match touchline ban in his role as manager of Northern League football team Ashington. Harmison confronted the referee after one of his players was sent off in a 1–0 defeat against Bishop Auckland. (2016)

8

BIG NUMBERS

Almost five hundred runs were scored without a wicket falling in a Hampshire League match at Gosport. The Hall brothers, Kieron and Chris, took Wildern Mansbridge to 243 without loss but the Farehaven openers, Mark Williams and Jason Murdoch, gave their team a ten-wicket victory. All four scored centuries. (2002)

Ezrafiq Andul Aziz scored 303 off 75 balls – including 30 sixes and 26 fours – to help Johore crush Labuan by 598 runs in a Malaysian Schools Sports Council match in Kota Baru. Labuan replied with 22 all out. (2003)

Mali Richards, the 19-year-old son of Sir Vivian, hit 319, the highest score in the ninety-year history of the Leeward Islands tournament, for Antigua & Barbuda in a three-day match against the US & British Virgin Islands at St John's. In reply to the hosts' 789, the Virgin Islands made 47. (2003)

United Cricket Club of the Northern California League scored 630 for five in a 45-over match against Bay Area. Opener Shabbir Mohammad scored 353 in a 449-run win. (2006)

Two Under-13 batsmen in Hyderabad, India, Manoj Kumar and Mohammed Shaibaz Tumbi, shared an unbroken first-wicket stand of 721 for St Peter's High School against St Philip's. The partnership is the highest on record in any form of cricket, beating the 664 by the young Sachin Tendulkar and Vinod Kambli in 1987–88. Tumbi hit 324 and Kumar 320. St Philip's were then bowled out for 21. The umpires described the record as genuine but added that St Philip's were playing their first game. "There were more than a hundred overthrows and the team did not possess any cricketing strategy, as was evident by the field placements," one said. (2006)

In an Under-13 match in Sri Lanka, Bandarawela Central scored 553 for three in 46 overs; their opponents, Pussellakanda Vidyalaya, were then bowled out for three. Following on, they improved, reaching 31 to lose by an innings and 519. (2010)

In the Under-14 Giles Shield in Mumbai, Rizvi Springfield beat Christ Church, Byculla, by an innings and 808 runs (869 v 22 and 39). (2011)

The waiting list for the Melbourne Cricket Club was reported to have surpassed the population of Hobart, and stands at 217,000. It was estimated that it took between twenty-two and twenty-three years to join the 61,500 full members and gain full privileges at major MCG occasions. About 3,000 vacancies were occurring each year, but the list was growing inexorably because there were also 15,000 new applicants. However, the club had lost contact with many of those waiting because they moved so often. (2012)

Settle beat Stacksteads in Division Two of the Ribblesdale League by 452 runs in a 45-over match. Settle captain Nick Cokell scored 275 not out in a total of 467 for one. Stacksteads were then bowled out for 15, the lowest score in the league since 1931. "I'd never even scored a century before," said Cokell. "To be fair, Stacksteads were gracious in defeat." (2012)

In Calcutta, Nava Nalanda High School beat Gyan Bharati Vidyapith by 812 runs in the Mayor's Cup inter-school tournament. Nava Nalanda scored 844 for two in 38 overs, which included 227 penalty runs for a slow over rate. Second-top scorer was Sreyas Banerjee with 193. Their opponents were all out for 32. (2016)

9

BOWLERS

Alex Kelly, a 17-year-old schoolboy, took ten wickets for no runs – all bowled – in 27 deliveries, bowling medium-pace for Bishop Auckland against Newton Aycliffe in the Durham County Junior League. Kelly came on to bowl when the score was 36 for nought; it was soon 47 all out. "I have never played so well before," he said, "and the only thing I can think of was that I was angry because I'd been dropped to No. 4 in the batting order." John Wisden is the only player to have bowled all ten in first-class cricket. (1994)

Emma Liddell, a 15-year-old Sydney schoolgirl, took ten for nought for Metropolitan East against Metropolitan West. All her victims were bowled. (1996)

Phil Hutchings, 65, of Abbotsbury, Dorset, claimed a hat-trick after taking two wickets with his last deliveries of 1996 and another with his first of 1997 – against the same opponents, Burley. (1997)

Darren Bloomfield of the Essex club Tiptree United claimed a hat-trick spread over three separate matches. Bloomfield, an occasional off-spinner, was brought on with nine wickets down against Chappel & Wakes Colne, and ended the innings first ball. The same thing happened two weeks later against Cavaliers. The following week he was brought on earlier against Dedham, and took a wicket first ball again. He said he hoped the club might start bowling him more regularly. (1997)

Richard Shotton, 32, took a hat-trick with his first three balls for his new team, Hengrove Second Eleven, in a Bristol & District League match against Pucklechurch. Shotton, a part-time bowler, had only recently moved into the area. (1998)

In Staffordshire, Andrew Dale, 19, took a hat-trick with the first three balls of a match for Sandyford Second Eleven against Rode Park. His victims included the 61-year-old former Northamptonshire all-rounder Brian Crump. (1999)

George Digweed, 35, eight-time winner of the world clay pigeon shooting championship, took eight for nought in five overs playing for Pett against Ashburnham in the Hastings Midweek Cup. Ashburnham were bowled out for 26. The assistant editor of *Clay Shooting* magazine said Digweed was the best clay pigeon shooter there had ever been: no one else had ever won more than three titles. The captain of Pett, John Osborn, said Digweed was only allowed to open the bowling because one of the regulars was away. (1999)

David Morton of the Bayside Muddies took all ten wickets for nought as the Ranatungas were dismissed for 20 in the Brisbane Warehouse Cricket Association B3 South Saturday competition. (1999)

A 46-year-old bricklayer who had only been playing competitive cricket for two years took five wickets in an over for Redbourn Rogues in the Scunthorpe Pub and Club Friendly League. In his second over at Cemetery Road against Messingham Crown, Tony Maltby took a wicket with his first ball, and then with the last four. (1999)

A no-ball cost Matthew Whiley of Nottinghamshire £5,000 in a competition at Lord's to find Britain's fastest young bowler. Whiley recorded the fastest delivery – 86.5mph against 86.2 by Yorkshire's Matthew Hoggard – but overstepped by about half an inch. (2000) *Whiley went on to play 18 first-class matches for Nottinghamshire and Leicestershire; Hoggard played 67 Tests.*

Tom Matthews, a schoolboy playing for Fakenham Third Eleven, bowled out Snettisham's Second Eleven with figures of 3–2–4–10. The four, a dropped slip catch that sped to the rope, constituted Snettisham's only runs. Under West Norfolk League rules, 15-year-old Matthews would have been restricted to a five-over spell because of his age. (2001)

Changing ends after an unprofitable spell, Sam Collins took two hat-tricks for the Kent side Band of Brothers in the space of seven balls. The Arabs, the club founded by the late E. W. Swanton, plunged from 186 for four to 187 all out, yet still won the match. (2002)

Craig Primmer, a 6 foot 5 inch pace bowler from New Zealand, took seven for nought in nine balls, including two hat-tricks, for Pagham in Sussex against the Crawley team, Ram. In 2003, he took four in five balls, with a hat-trick, against Clymping. (2005)

Mark Mansell of Kidderminster Victoria in the Birmingham League had figures of 11–11–0–3 against Coventry & North Warwickshire. (2007)

Seam bowler Scott Babot of Wainuiomata, New Zealand, took five wickets in five balls against Johnsonville, spread over two weekends. He took a hat-trick to wrap up the first innings one Saturday and then took two wickets with the first two balls of the second innings a week later. (2008)

Chris Prestt, 21, of Stoketeignhead took all the Dartington & Totnes wickets in a South Devon League fixture, even though it was a limited-overs match in which he was restricted to nine overs. Prestt took ten for 20 in 52 balls, as the opposition crumbled to 38 all out. (2009)

In Hertfordshire, two cricketers broke the same club's bowling records on the same day. Brad Klosterman took nine for 15 for the Leverstock Green first team, only to hear later that Imran Iqbal had taken nine for 13 for the seconds that afternoon. (2009)

James Vallois, 17, of Aztec Springfield took six wickets, all bowled, in an eight-ball over in a Jersey evening league match against Optimus Colts (WW.W.WWW). Colts went from 30 for two to 30 for eight before recovering to 64 all out; Aztec won by ten wickets. (2010)

Left-arm paceman Rhys Yorke, bowling for South Brisbane's second-grade team, took two hat-tricks on successive days: three lbws ("all plumb," he said) against Valleys, before another against Sunshine Coast in a cup-tie on Sunday. (2013)

In South London, Kato Harris had figures of 5.2–5–1–9 for Alleyn & Honor Oak's Sunday team, the best analysis in the club's history. Harris was stunned by his performance, since he had been suffering from the yips: "I just completely lost it," he said. "I went from my worst game to my best game in the space of a week." (2014)

Tommy Stewart, a 13-year-old pupil at Hugh Sexey's School in Somerset, bowled out the Gryphon School in an Under-14 match and finished with 5–3–2–10. Stewart gave the credit to the school's head of cricket, Tom Balch: "I was disappointed to have got out to a poor shot when I batted, and Mr Balch told me to channel my frustration into my bowling." (2014)

Alex Smeeth took nine for ten off 23 balls as Werrington bowled out Newquay for 14 in the Cornwall Premier League. The last four wickets fell to Smeeth's last four balls, and none of the nine involved a fielder – six were bowled and three lbw. (2014)

Gareth Davies, 19, took all ten Buckley wickets bowling for Mold in a Second Eleven match in the North Wales League. His figures were 12–7–11–10. He claimed the final wicket with an lbw decision from a clubmate-umpire off the final ball of his allotted twelve overs. "It was dead in line," Davies insisted. "I had gone up for five or six lbws and, to be fair to him, he didn't just give them." (2015)

Aled Carey, 29, took six wickets in an over for Golden Point against East Ballarat in Victoria. Carey, unable to take a wicket in his first eight overs, changed that dramatically in the ninth. The last three were all bowled as East Ballarat were all out for 40. (2017)

Thomas Perez took six wickets in six balls in Tuggerangong's final two-day game of the season, against St Edmunds in the Australian Capital Territory's colts competition. Perez had match figures of 12 for 26; he had previously taken four wickets all season. (2017)

Seam bowler Curtis Groves took five wickets in his first eight balls of first-team cricket for Immanuel College, Adelaide, against Sacred Heart. (2017)

Inswing bowler Tony Wilkinson, 40, took six wickets in an over for Holmfirth Second Eleven against Birkby Rose Hill in the Huddersfield League. He was making his first appearance of the season after a single net session, which he described as "horrendous", and his first ball of the day was smashed into the bowling green for six. Wilkinson finished with 5.4–1–20–8 as the opposition were bowled out for 51 to lose by five wickets. "It was all a bit of a blur," he said. (2017)

In the Derbyshire League, Alrewas opening bowler Loz Cousins had figures of 7.3–7–0–9 in a Third Eleven match against Brailsford & Ednaston. Their openers put on 16 but the team were bowled out for 31. (2017)

Luke Robinson took six wickets in an over, all clean bowled, in an Under-13 match for Philadelphia Cricket Club, County Durham, against Langley Park. "Time stood still and I thought, 'is this really happening?'" said the bowler's end umpire, Stephen Robinson, who also happened to be the bowler's father. Luke's mother Helen was scoring. The opposition were bowled out for 18 and Philadelphia won by 58 runs. (2017)

Nick Gooden of Yallourn North took eight for two in ten balls – including five in five and a separate hat-trick – against Latrobe in a third-grade match in Central Gippsland, Victoria. (2017)

BOYS WILL BE BOYS

A twenty-stone man streaked across the pitch during a match between Cockerton and Durham for a £15 bet. (1993)

Players from Scholes Cricket Club, near Holmfirth, Yorkshire, had an impromptu match stopped by police at 4.30am because they were "inappropriately dressed" – they were wearing only boots and socks. The team had been at a late-night party. (2000)

Players from Ben Rhydding Cricket Club, near Ilkley, Yorkshire, drew their largest crowd of the year – a dozen passing motorists – when they played a night fixture illuminated by car headlights. All the players were naked, although the umpire wore his white coat. Play lasted an hour until the police arrived after a complaint. Club captain Andrew Jennings insisted he was proud of his players. "It was the last night of the season

and we'd had a few too many beers. We just thought: 'Get 'em off and let's get on with it.' It was freezing. There were men of all shapes and sizes. It's what sport is all about." (2000)

Police arrested nine white cricketers for dancing nude in the rain on the cricket pitch at Hwange, Zimbabwe, during celebrations marking the anniversary of the Wankie Cricket Club. Inspector Andrew Phiri said: "They were all playing cricket, following the normal cricket rules, and when it started raining all the officials and players left the ground. All of a sudden these nine undressed, rushed back and started dancing round naked… Nude! Nude!" He added that some spectators took photographs. (2004)

Residents of Carholme Road, Lincoln, were woken at 4am by six naked men, believed to be students, playing cricket in the street. (2007)

Thirty Colombo schoolboys were arrested after climbing the walls of a nearby girls' school and demanding money to support their "Big Match". The contests between rival schools are an important part of Sri Lankan cricket tradition and have long been accompanied by a student-rag atmosphere. However, police had specifically issued a warning through the media that girls' schools were off limits. The boys were given a further warning and released without charge. (2012)

Hampshire insisted that a man who walked naked into a supermarket at 4.20am and tried to buy a bottle of vodka was not one of their players. After examining CCTV footage, the club denied reports that the streaker was a member of their Second Eleven squad, who were staying at the next-door hotel in Ashford, Kent. (2013)

DECISIONS, DECISIONS

Ian Harris, of the Veryan club near Truro, who continued playing after losing a leg in a farm accident in 1987, was told by the Cornwall Umpires' Association that he could not bat with a runner under Law 2.5, which covers only injuries received during the match. MCC said their interpretation was over-zealous, and the umpires relented. (1993)

The match between Methodists and Sandown Park in the Dandenong & District Cricket Association, outside Melbourne, was declared a draw ten days after it finished, following four hearings, when local officials finally sought advice from MCC. Methodists lost their ninth wicket to the last available ball and Sandown claimed victory because they knew the last man was missing. (1994)

A ball bowled by Chris Thomas at Trimdon, County Durham, hit and killed a swallow and was deflected on to batsman Joe Hall's stumps. After a long conference, the umpires ruled that the delivery was missing the stumps, declared the ball dead as well as the swallow, and said Hall was not out. (1994)

Slow left-armer James Didcote was no-balled twice under Law 40.1, playing for Glamorgan Colts against Llandovery College, because the wicketkeeper's peaked cap was protruding in front of the stumps. The keeper was Gareth Jones, 17, whose father Eifion kept for Glamorgan. (1995)

In a prep-school match between Northbridge and St Paul's, Northbridge were given an extra "for too much chatter in the short-leg cordon while J. Edwards was bowling his hat-trick ball". (1996)

A Hampshire League match was declared void because Southampton Travellers fielded twelve men against Hamble Aerostructures. The mistake was only discovered at the drinks interval when one of the fielders complained that he had missed out. (1997)

Two clubs in the North Yorkshire & South Durham League, Norton and Preston-on-Tees B, were deemed to have lost matches they called off on the day of the funeral of Diana, Princess of Wales. The decision cost Norton a chance of winning the league; their opponents, Darlington, had said they were happy to rearrange the game. No major sporting fixtures took place that day. Frank Cook, the local Labour MP, called the decision "diabolical". (1997)

The Western Province innings in a day/night match against Free State at Newlands ended without a not-out batsman at the crease. Province were batting first when Paul Kirsten was run out with a ball to go. Since the new batsman would have gone to the non-striker's end anyway, umpire Dave Orchard thought he was doing everyone a favour by letting Kirsten stay out there, although he confirmed he was definitely out. However, the other batsman, Ashwell Prince, was run out off the final ball. John Commins, despite never reaching the crease, was officially recorded as not out 0. It was unclear what would have happened had Kirsten been run out again. (1999)

A Hurstpierpoint tailender, Joe Andrews, sent a slow half-volley from an Ardingly College bowler over long-on for what appeared to be the winning six off the final ball of a cup-tie in Sussex. However, there was doubt whether the ball bounced on the line or marginally in front. The umpires admitted their confusion, and so the teams, in the interests of the game's "true spirit", agreed to a replay. (2001)

Shane Warne, still chasing his maiden century four years later, was told he had been wrongfully denied the chance of scoring one in a Test in 2001, when he was caught in the outfield for 99 against New Zealand at Perth. Channel 9 had unearthed previously unseen footage showing that the crucial delivery, bowled by Daniel Vettori, should have been called a no-ball, and played it at the Allan Border Medal dinner. Asked how he felt, Warne said: "We're on TV so I can't swear." (2005)

Actor David Troughton, father of Warwickshire batsman Jim and a Level Four umpire, said umpiring was far more stressful than acting: "It's all ad lib," he explained. (2008)

DOPE

Players from the Nerrena club in Victoria were served green-speckled cupcakes for tea by rivals Inverloch. They later claimed the cakes were laced with marijuana. "I thought, gee, this is pretty good, they usually feed us crap," said Nerrena player Tim Clark. He ate five, other players also tucked in, and then their game went to pieces. One player took nearly twenty minutes to put on his pads, while two others broke out in hysterical laughter and fled the pitch for drinks of water. Nerrena lost by 50 runs and ended up relegated. Inverloch secretary Ian Smith said the allegations were all rumours. "This is just a witch-hunt," he said. (2005)

Hashish stuffed into cricket balls was seized by agents at Frankfurt Airport. (2006)

Senior Sri Lankan prison officials flew to Malaysia on an eight-day cricket tour. Well-informed sources said the tour was sponsored by jailed drug barons. (2006)

Whakamana, the new museum in Dunedin devoted to cannabis, is planning a special exhibition called "Hit for Six". Timed to coincide with the Test against West Indies, it explores the connection between cricket and dope-smoking: "Cannabis and cricket just seem to go together for some reason," said curator Abe Gray. "It's hands-down the favourite sport among Kiwi stoners." New Zealand Cricket declined to comment. (2013)

West Midlands police have handed over heat lamps, confiscated after raids on cannabis farms, to Warwickshire to help the (legal) grass grow at Edgbaston. (2014)

West Indies opener Lendl Simmons had four holes drilled into his bat by US customs officials looking for drugs. Simmons was travelling with his Caribbean Premier League side, Guyana Amazon Warriors, and his team-mate Jimmy Neesham tweeted a picture of the damaged bat. There was no suggestion Simmons was under personal suspicion. (2014)

Former England all-rounder Chris Lewis, 47, has been released from prison after serving just under half a thirteen-year sentence for drug smuggling. He said worries about money had led to his attempt to import £140,000 worth of dissolved cocaine into the UK. "I became afraid of what the future held, and at that point the thinking went awry," he said in an interview with the Professional Cricketers' Association. "I made choices. They were the wrong choices, and I say sorry for them." (2015)

EMBARRASSMENT

Thieves failed in an attempt to steal the artificial wicket at Coaver Cricket Club, Exeter, when they discovered it was too heavy to carry. (1994)

The pub named after Geoffrey Boycott in Dewsbury, Yorkshire, returned to its old name of The Park after Boycott's conviction for assaulting a girlfriend. "From then on women just stopped coming in," said landlady Anne-Marie Higgins. There was also a "Boycott the Boycott" protest. The sign was burned, and the ashes kept behind the bar. (2000) *The name of the pub is, alas, no longer an issue: according to the local branch of CAMRA, the building is now used as a pre-school nursery.*

A fraud trial in Devon was stopped after the judge revealed that he and one of the witnesses had once played cricket together. (2001)

Asia's largest prison has removed the name of Manoj Prabhakar from one of its jail blocks. Cited during his heyday as a role model for inmates at Tihar jail in New Delhi, the former Indian Test all-rounder had been embroiled in the match-fixing scandal. (2001)

Shane Warne was fined and banned from driving on British roads for three months for reaching 120mph on the M1 in Derbyshire. The case had been adjourned nine times because of problems serving papers on Warne, who admitted the offence in a letter to Ilkeston magistrates. "Thank you for your patience," he wrote. "I'm sorry I was going too fast in your country. I love playing cricket in England." (2002)

St Buryan's had 33 on the board after the first over of their Cornwall League Premier Division fixture against Meheniot. J. Sedgley bowled 25 wides. (2003)

A school governor complained after watching a fellow spectator start marking GCSE exam papers at Chelmsford during an Essex–Warwickshire one-day game. Carole Nadin said she saw him pass the papers to his friends, who laughed when they read the answers. (2003)

In a blind tasting organised on Channel 4 by chef Gordon Ramsay, Sir Ian Botham described a £106 bottle of Montrachet as undrinkable, and said he preferred a bottle of plonk from a vineyard owned by Barry Manilow. Botham avoided total humiliation by recognising his own brand of wine. (2007)

Northern Rock, the bank nationalised by the British government to save it from collapse, handed £150,000 to its chief executive's cricket club months before the £27 billion rescue. Sunderland Cricket Club, where Adam Applegarth was a keen player, received a £100,000 donation and a £50,000 loan. (2008)

One of the big, bailed-out High Street banks asked not to have advertising signs in front of its hospitality boxes at the 2009 Ashes Tests to avoid criticism for wasting public money. (2008)

An In Memoriam notice appeared in a Sussex parish magazine after the Worthing-based St Symphorians team were beaten by a side from their twin town of München, Germany. The Germans barely understood the Laws and did not immediately realise they had won. (2008)

Fast bowler Zaid Mir of Port Qasim had to be removed from the attack after conceding 31 runs without bowling a single legal delivery. Zaid bowled ten consecutive no-balls in a Pakistani Twenty20 match against Karachi Gymkhana, giving away two each for the no-balls and 11 in free hits. The umpires kindly agreed to let his team-mate Shadab Kabir finish the over on the grounds that Zaid had a leg strain. (2008)

Citizen watches ran a press ad featuring Kevin Pietersen the day after injury forced his withdrawal from the Ashes. The slogan was: "Unstoppable? Kevin Pietersen is." (2009)

Rob Pritchard scored his first runs in two years for Ingatestone & Fryerning in Essex after eight successive ducks. Pritchard, regarded as a competent middle-order batsman, had been renamed "Paddles" by team-mates. "We cringe when he comes into bat," said Matthew Taylor. Pritchard promised to end the sequence against Great Totham, but was hit in the face fifth ball and retired hurt. However, he returned, nose bloodied, and scored five not out. (2013)

Businessman Michael Whitaker left his car unlocked overnight, and found a man sleeping in it next morning. A police officer was called and woke the intruder, who turned out to be Nottinghamshire's Zimbabwean batsman, Brendan Taylor. "Neither myself, the police, nor Brendan knew what to do," said Whitaker. "I don't think he knew where he was, but he was very apologetic, and it quickly became clear that it was very innocent." A spokesman for Nottinghamshire Police said: "We attended the scene but concluded that no offence had been committed." (2015)

One of the purest gold nuggets ever found, the Maitland Bar, was rediscovered, having been unwittingly used for years by New South Wales Treasury officials as a wicket. The bar, NSW Premier Mike Baird explained, had been entrusted to the Treasury some years previously: "Someone studiously decided they'd place it in a box. The problem was they forgot to tell anyone, and that box became used for hallway cricket." The bar has a gold content of 8.87kg. "My good friends in Treasury – I love them dearly, but that was not their finest moment," Baird sighed. (2015)

In Lancashire, Farnworth Cricket Club continued their tradition of burning topical effigies as Bonfire Night guys... by choosing a cricketer. As ever, groundsman Jack Greasley, who has previously chosen crooked MPs, fat cat bankers and the irritating opera singer from the Go Compare advert, made the decision. "This year our senior squad were in two major finals and came away with no trophies at all, so there were a lot of disappointed people," explained Greasley. "Because of that, I thought this year we would burn a cricketer. I do like being a little bit controversial with these things, and it has certainly got people talking." (2016)

Jaipur traffic police pulled down a hoarding making use of Indian bowler Jasprit Bumrah's infamous no-ball against Pakistan in the Champions Trophy final. The sign warned motorists not to cross the line at pedestrian crossings alongside a shot of Bumrah crossing the line at The Oval, adding: "You know it can be costly." "This is how much respect you get after giving your best for your country," tweeted Bumrah. "We only intended to create more awareness about traffic rules. You are a youth icon & an inspiration," the police replied before surrendering. Bumrah had apparently dismissed Fakhar Zaman on three; Fakhar went to make a match-winning 114. (2017)

A total of 136 wides were bowled in 65.3 overs during an Under-19 women's championship match in India between Nagaland and Manipur in Dhanbad, India. Manipur bowled 94 of them. "Forget about being accurate, balls were barely reaching the other end as well, which raises questions about the preparedness," an official said. "The gap in standards between the top sides and the rest is huge in women's cricket." Both states are in north-east India where cricket is less developed than elsewhere in the country. (2017)

... AND A FEW WEEKS LATER

The Nagaland women's Under-19 team were bowled out for two by Kerala. Their only runs – one off the bat and a wide – came during the six-over opening partnership. The team then collapsed in 11.4 overs. Head coach Hokaito Zhimoni said that Nagaland, a small state, had been forced to advertise for players and had had hardly any time to practise. "Now the girls have got a sense of where they stand and where they need to improve," he said. (2017)

... BUT ALL BAD THINGS COME TO AN END

Ash Tree Cricket Club, based in Prestbury, Cheshire, won a match on their annual overseas tour for the first time in 35 years, beating Sir William Hoste Cricket Club by two runs on the Croatian island of Vis. Though the club claim a reasonable record at home, their touring record became a standing joke. "We used to share our record with the team we were playing," said chairman Mark Crook. "But they never believed us and thought it was a ploy." The team (average age: 55) returned to form next day and lost the rematch. (2017)

ENTHUSIASTIC

Ernie Jones, 46, set up house in the scorebox at Crewe & Nantwich Cricket Club, moving in a bed and wiring up lights to a car battery. (1993)

A judge who asked to borrow a television to watch the Lord's Test against New Zealand while the jury was out at Maidstone Crown Court was refused by security guards: they were watching Royal Ascot. (1994)

Sir Tim Rice, accepting an Oscar for Best Original Song – in the Disney film *The Lion King* – told the audience in Hollywood: "I'd also like to thank Denis Compton, a boyhood hero of mine." A spokesman for the Academy of Motion Picture Arts and Sciences said: "We don't know who Denis Compton is. He doesn't appear to be at Disney Studios or have anything to do with *The Lion King*." (1995)

Graham Yallop, the former captain of Australia, was sacked from his post as manager of the Australian National Watersports Centre for playing club cricket at weekends. He was awarded $A12,500 compensation after an industrial relations court decided that his dismissal was "harsh, unjust and unreasonable". (1995)

Thirty cardboard cut-out Mike Athertons, produced for a pub promotion, went missing from a warehouse in Leeds. (1995)

Rick Sidwell, 33, of Fareham, Hampshire, smoked 12,800 cigarettes at a cost of £1,700 to win two free £20 tickets to the Benson and Hedges Cup final. (1995)

The Hawks, a Leeds-based club, advertised for "fun-loving" women in Bournemouth to meet them on their seaside tour. They received thirty replies. (1995)

A pair of shoes belonging to the Sri Lankan captain, Arjuna Ranatunga, went missing and were replaced by a brand new pair when he visited a former Sri Lankan president's house and left them outside as a mark of respect. Police discovered a woman fan had taken them as a souvenir, and had put the new pair down instead. Ranatunga did not press charges. (1996)

A former Miss Sri Lanka was caught by security officials hiding in a bush outside the Hotel Lanka Oberoi during the Singer one-day tournament, where unprecedented security was in operation. It was alleged that she had just visited one of the players' bedrooms. (1996)

Seventeen ships were left waiting outside the harbour in Colombo because half the port's 16,000 workers stayed away from work to watch the India v Sri Lanka one-day international. (1996)

Twenty-eight prisoners broke down two doors and walked out of a minimum-security jail in Guyana in protest after guards turned off a radio broadcast of the First Test between Australia and West Indies. (1997)

Basdeo Debideen, who was under sentence of death in the Port-of-Spain state prison, wrote to *The Cricketer* magazine asking for a pen-pal. (1997)

The Sri Lankan Health Department acquired a new blood-testing machine for use by the country's hospitals. The Health Minister, A. H. M. Fowzie, said that under the old system various errors occurred, including a case when the technician was watching a cricket match on TV while testing a male patient and told him he was pregnant. (1997)

Geoffrey Boycott's TV commentaries turned him into a cult figure in India. One group of schoolboys were given six of the best by their

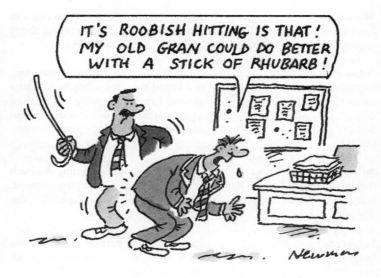

headmaster for constantly imitating Boycott and describing everything as "roobish". (1997)

Village cricketers at Over, Cambridgeshire, continued playing in honour of lifelong supporter Sid Wright who died, aged 86, while watching a game. "It's what Sid would have wanted," said a club spokesman. (1998)

A Sri Lankan inquest decided that R. G. Ranasinghe of Wattegama had died from "a heart attack caused by excessive happiness" after watching Sri Lanka beat England in the Oval Test. (1998)

An impromptu game of cricket in the gents' toilet at the Dutch Open Championships led to English badminton internationals Peter Knowles and Colin Haughton being suspended for ten weeks and six weeks respectively. They played with a cleaner's brush and a bar of soap; Knowles reacted angrily when there were complaints. (1998)

Chris Gent, chief executive of Vodafone, initiated a £36 billion merger with the US mobile phone company Airtouch on his own mobile while watching the Ashes Test at Sydney. (1999)

Rupert Rucker and Susie Peel, who got married in Edensor, Derbyshire, received a £50 bet from a friend as a wedding present, which will net them £1.4 million if their first-born son opens the batting for England at Lord's and takes a hat-trick in the same match. (1999)

A Calcutta schoolteacher, Tejesh Adhikary, has invented a new game called "Reading Cricket" to help cricket-crazy students improve their literacy. Two teams are given separate unseen texts. The batting side has to read out a passage, and the fielding side appeals to an umpire if it feels a word is mispronounced or omitted. The batsman gets one run for reading a column correctly, and a boundary for pronouncing correctly any word in a foreign language. "This is a unique method for developing a flair for reading among school students," Adhikary said. (2000)

Film star Tom Cruise was taken to the Sydney Cricket Ground by director Sam Mendes to watch a one-day international. "He didn't know anything about cricket," said Mendes. "I told him about Warne and Tendulkar, how amazing Bradman was, and that Mark Taylor had declared when he was 334 not out, equal with Bradman's Australian Test record. Tom was so moved he was practically in tears. He enjoyed it so much he hired the box himself for a match the next day." (2000)

Luen Man, 34, has been commuting from Switzerland to play village matches at Kirkby Overblow, Yorkshire. (2000)

Lynton & Lynmouth Cricket Club in Devon were "racking brains for fund-raising ideas to replace the roller and mower" when Christopher Ondaatje, the retired businessman who owns the nearby Glenthorne Estate, donated £100,000 to the club in addition to setting up a trust fund in its favour. The Lynton & Lynmouth players, he said, "embody everything that is good and noble about cricket in England". (2001)

Charlie Watts, the Rolling Stones drummer, nominated John Arlott's commentary of Jim Laker taking nineteen wickets against Australia at Old Trafford in 1956 as one of his *Desert Island Discs* on Radio 4. (2001)

Stuart Jeffrey, who had travelled 9,000 miles from Perth to watch the Headingley Test, hired a 40-foot crane to watch the game after learning that the ground was sold out. (2001)

The imprisoned author and politician, Lord Archer, paid more than £1,000 to obtain enough turf from the dug-up Lord's outfield to re-lay his back garden in Cambridgeshire. Archer was later suspended from MCC for seven years having been jailed for four years for perjury and perverting the course of justice. (2002)

About two hundred tourists paid 20 rand (£1.40) each on the first two days of an exhibition showing the wreckage of the plane in which the former South African captain Hansie Cronje died. The remnants of the Hawker Siddeley 748 freighter were laid out on the floor of a warehouse in Mossel Bay. (2002)

Interviewed on *Tonight*, the US TV chat show hosted by Jay Leno, the actor Keanu Reeves, fresh from filming in Australia, amazed both audience and compère by mounting a stirring defence of cricket. "But doesn't it go on for days and days?" wondered Leno, amid studio laughter. "Cricket's cool," insisted Reeves. "In five days you have time to, like, get real into it." (2003)

Doug Robertson, a 60-year-old teacher from Bexhill, Sussex, visited each of the eighteen first-class county headquarters in eighteen days. Rain at Derby and an early finish at Worcester prevented him from seeing cricket played every day, but in each instance the players signed a bat as evidence of his visit. He raised £6,000 for charity. (2003)

Ramanlal Pathak, a Sanskrit scholar from Vadodara, India, has spent seven years assembling a cricket vocabulary to freshen the appeal of "a dying language". A batsman is *bat-dhar*, runs translate to *gaccha* or *dhavan*. *Pashya pashya chowka* means "another glorious shot for four". (2003)

Comedian Jimmy Tarbuck included a tape of the *Test Match Special* "legover" giggle between Brian Johnston and Jonathan Agnew in 1991 in his selection of eight records for *Desert Island Discs*. (2004)

A London-based Pakistani businessman, named as M. Jamshaid, offered the Pakistan Cricket Board a million pounds if it would pick him to play against India. The board said it first treated the offer as a joke, but when it received repeated requests it told Jamshaid to spend the money on cricketing development in his home area of Pakistan. "You might not be a deserving cricketer but you are definitely a millionaire," said the board, "and what you need to do is to spend the amount on a noble cause." (2005)

New Zealand Cricket roped off an area at the Basin Reserve, Wellington, to keep flagwaving supporter Sonny Shaw off TV screens. Shaw habitually parked himself near the sightscreen, sometimes stripped to the waist, waving a flag. Sky TV producer James Cameron made the request after complaints from cameramen. "It was to create a cleaner shot," he explained. (2005)

Carl Ferris, 15, was banned from classes at Westfield Community School, Yeovil, because he refused to get rid of his two-tone spiky haircut, chosen in imitation of Kevin Pietersen, his hero. Carl's father Roy said: "It's an invasion of human rights." Pietersen by this time had shaved his head. (2006)

Hertfordshire village cricketer Jim Young, 57, batted on after he had a heart attack because he was desperate to make a half-century. Playing for Westmill against a Bishop's Stortford side, he retired briefly, then came out again with a runner before being left stranded on 48 when the team were all out. Only then was he taken to hospital. "I think I was a bit of an idiot really," he admitted later. (2006)

Rock band McFly set off the fire alarm playing cricket backstage before a concert at the Sheffield Arena. The ball hit the alarm and caused a two-hour delay in preparations. (2006)

A policewoman at Baker Street station, London, briefly confiscated a cricket ball from Chris Hurd, 28, an accountant and occasional leg-spinner. Hurd was holding the ball on the escalator when he was stopped and questioned for ten minutes. He said he was taking the ball to work because he was excited about the start of the Ashes: "All I was doing was holding it." (2006)

An 11-year-old boy from Leicestershire, Callum Church, broke the BBC *Junior Mastermind* record for the highest number of points in his specialist subject by getting all nineteen questions right about Andrew Flintoff. However, he did less well on general knowledge and so lost the final by one point to an opponent who chose the Adventures of Tintin. Callum said he had met Flintoff once and that he was "a lot bigger than you expect him to be and very, very nice". (2007)

Sarun Sharma, 23, from Mango, near Jamshedpur, offered one of his kidneys for sale so that he could go to watch the World Cup in the Caribbean. "Anybody can survive with one kidney," he said, "but you will never get the opportunity to watch India win the Cup in the West Indies." Police said his offer was illegal. (2007)

Glamorgan batsman Mike Powell buried one of his ribs – removed during an operation – beneath the turf at the club's headquarters. "I am glad that part of me will be at Sophia Gardens for ever," he said. (2007)

Daniel Radcliffe, the 18-year-old star of the Harry Potter films, queued to get the autographs of Sachin Tendulkar and Andrew Strauss at the Lord's Test. Radcliffe said he had become hooked on cricket when watching Paul Collingwood's impassioned celebration after his double-century in the 2006–07 Adelaide Test. Radcliffe also said he had been having nightmares that Strauss was stalking him. (2007)

The Rolling Stones' list of demands to venues hosting their Bigger Bang tour included de-thorned white roses, a room for their snooker table, and a TV with information about which channel is showing the cricket. "That is the channel we need most of all," the list says. (2007)

Bob Marchant interrupted a family holiday in southern Spain to fly home for a match in Hampshire, but his team, Fareham & Crofton, won before he got a chance to bat. His brother Graham commutes from

Dumfries in Scotland to play for the side but said he now plans to give that up: "Some of our players miss games because someone's having a party or something," he noted sadly. (2008)

League cricketer Mark Aspin and his bride Naomi celebrated their wedding with a reception on a cricket pitch at Bolton Abbey, Yorkshire. Naomi, who is training to be an umpire, said: "Rather than champagne and canapés we had a traditional tea of sandwiches, scones, tea and lemonade and played a little cricket while being serenaded by a string quartet. It was the perfect English cricket afternoon." (2008)

Room 374 of the Pegasus Hotel in Kingston, Jamaica – where Bob Woolmer died during the 2007 World Cup – has become a bizarre tourist destination. "We have had quite a few occasions where people have asked to stay in the Woolmer room," said hotel manager Eldon Bremner, "and others have asked to stay on the same floor." (2008)

A shopkeeper from Uttar Pradesh sold his shop and its entire stock of CDs and cassettes to pay for a trip to Mahendra Singh Dhoni's home town of Ranchi after his fiancée said she would only marry him if he could offer proof that he had met Dhoni. He spent a month in Ranchi, sometimes sleeping rough, awaiting the return of the cricketer, who eventually heard the story, took pity, and posed for a picture. (2009)

Stanley Johnson, a cricket fan who watched more than two hundred overseas Tests, is to have his ashes scattered round his twelve favourite grounds, from Accrington to Sydney. Johnson died in New Zealand, aged 72, during a Test against Pakistan. An Oxford-educated accountant who spoke eight languages, he had retired aged 44 and devoted himself to watching cricket. In his will he told his friends to drink beer at each ground wearing a special T-shirt with the words "The Stan Johnson Ashes Tour". (2010)

Students in Moradabad, Uttar Pradesh, built a 45-foot cricket bat to try to inspire India to victory in the World Cup. The bat was scrapped when they discovered Pakistani supporters had built a 50-foot model in Karachi. (2011)

Staff in Whitehall's Department of Communities and Local Government accessed leading websites 54 million times in the previous month, according to a survey by officials. This included 383,000 hits for Cricinfo. (2012)

The Indian matrimonial site, shaadi.com, said its "millions" of member profiles showed 32.8% of men wanted a bride who was interested in cricket. Only 11.4% of women wanted cricket-loving grooms. (2013)

"Soul Limbo" by Booker T and the MGs, the BBC *Test Match Special* signature tune, is at No. 10 in the Co-operative Funeralcare's annual survey of British funeral music. "My Way" has been replaced at No. 1 by Monty Python's "Always Look on the Bright Side of Life". (2014)

Prisoners on remand in the Indian city of Guwahati have successfully petitioned a judge for the right to watch World Cup cricket. Justice Arup Kumar Goswami agreed that watching TV counted as a constitutional right, and added: "Prisoners need recreation for a healthy mind." They were already allowed to watch India matches, shown on the state channel Doordarshan, but not the other games, which were on cable. (2015)

Mike Jones, 45, said he was "living the dream" after being chosen as Essex's new Eddie the Eagle mascot. Jones, who works for Tesco in real life, was given the job after telling the club of his past experience: he and his girlfriend Cheryl dressed up as the Cookie Monster and Elmo from Sesame Street for a Seventies weekend at Butlins. (2016)

Brayden Hayes, 23, completed a 200-mile run across Tasmania in his underpants after joking on Facebook that he would do just that if the Hobart Hurricanes beat a record run total by the Melbourne Renegades. They did, and he did, raising nearly $20,000 for charities. (2017)

Amnesty International intervened after nineteen Pakistani cricket supporters were arrested for celebrating and chanting "Pakistan Zindabad" after Pakistan beat India in the Champions Trophy final. "These arrests are patently absurd," said Amnesty India programme director Asmita Basu. "Arresting someone for cheering a rival team clearly violates their right to freedom of expression." In the Himalayan city of Roorkee, local lawyers voted unanimously not to represent a man accused of putting a message on his Facebook page congratulating Pakistan. (2017)

Farmers near Delhi are turning their land into cricket grounds, staging Twenty20 matches for amateur players and charging far more than they ever earned growing wheat and mustard. Some villages now boast several of these mini-stadiums, complete with canteens and floodlights. With lights, grounds can stage up to five games a day for the city's growing middle-class. (2017)

... NOT ENTHUSIASTIC

A lorry driver drove off the A1 and parked on the pitch at Wansford, Cambridgeshire, to protest after 16-year-old Shaz Aftab had smashed his windscreen with a six. "He was very uptight and wouldn't move until we had exchanged insurance particulars," said umpire John Ingham. (1993)

Rye Cricket Club in Sussex, founded in 1754, has been told by the town council it must end the ancient practice of using Rye's official seal on its caps and sweaters. "The seal is being debased and degraded," said Councillor Frank Palmer. "People could use it to forge town council paper." The club chairman, Commander Colin Marsh, called the decision "pomposity and bureaucracy gone mad". (1997)

A coaching class for Under-16s in Nottinghamshire offered free by Sir Garry Sobers was cancelled when only nine youngsters signed up. Tom Meldrum, 12, one of the nine due to attend, said that when he mentioned the class to his friends they asked "Garry Who?" (1997)

Jennifer Christian drove on to the field in the middle of a match in Dorset, slid to a halt, flung her car keys at the man fielding in the gully and ran off, leaving their two children strapped in the car. Her husband Eric drove off after her and took no further part in the game, between the Dorchester Third Eleven and the Parley Montys from Wimborne. He refused to comment, but team-mates believed he had promised to look after the children that afternoon. (1998)

A leading Hindu sage has called on India to give up cricket because the manufacture of balls involves the slaughter of nine cows, which are sacred to Hindus, every day. Swami Nischalananda Saraswati Maharaj, custodian of the temple at Puri, said an alternative to cowhide should be found if the game was to continue. (1998)

Keith Jeffries of Aldwick hit a six which bounced off the top of a single-decker bus and then dented a red Jaguar at Sarisbury Green, Hampshire. "The Jaguar driver came over and said it was dangerous playing cricket so near a main road," reported Aldwick chairman Jim Smith. "It was pointed out to him that they had been playing here since 1774." (1999)

Peter Lee, a 65-year-old retired sailor, lost the chance to become the first to win £1 million on the ITV quiz *Who Wants To Be A Millionaire?* when he declined to answer the question: "Which county cricket side is based at Chester-le-Street?" Having answered fourteen previous questions correctly, he was given four options – Warwickshire, Durham, Northamptonshire or Leicestershire – but declined to try, which would have meant risking almost all his winnings, and accepted £500,000 instead. "I don't follow cricket," he said. Durham later invited him as their guest for a day. (2000)

The pitch at Fulmer, Buckinghamshire, has been sabotaged by being sprayed with weedkiller. Club captain David Jackson said: "Someone has got it in for us. We have our theories, but I will not say any more." Another villager, Clive Bushnell, said: "The problem is old women." (2005)

Winterbourne Bassett Cricket Club, Wiltshire, have been evicted from their home of twenty-three years by the field's owner, an Austrian count, apparently because the club refused to support him in an application to build houses on the land. Count Konrad Göss-Saurau was unavailable for comment. (2006)

The government of Madhya Pradesh, concerned that the glamour of cricket is leading youths astray, has proclaimed the traditional Indian pastime of *mallakambh* as its official state sport. Mallakambh is a form of gymnastics using a vertical pole polished with oil. "The government is trying to push the state back to the nineteenth century," said one cricket coach. (2007)

Councillors from twenty-eight villages in Jind, Haryana, issued a ban on playing cricket – or even mentioning the game – after India's World Cup failure. "This game is making the young boys go astray," said one official, Tewa Singh, adding that it led to gambling and fights. "It's better that the youngsters stay away from this game and don't even watch it." (2007)

Indian publishers have cut back production of student notebooks with cricketers on the cover after India's failure at the World Cup. Normally 60–70% of the books carry pictures of leading players, but demand has plummeted. "We have some old stock, but the kids do not want to buy them at all," said bookshop owner Abhijit Jahav. "They have been replaced by speeding cars." (2007)

Haworth West End Cricket Club in Yorkshire (founded 1900) has been told it cannot be given an electricity supply because it has no credit history. The club is sponsored by npower. (2007)

The batting sensation of South African women's cricket, 18-year-old Johmari Logtenberg, announced she was retiring to concentrate on golf. (2008)

Teachers have posted hundreds of complaints on an online forum about the idiocy of school inspectors from the British inspection body Ofsted. One PE teacher was allegedly told the lesson was "unsatisfactory as there were children doing nothing". The judgment was overturned after it was pointed out that the pupils were fielding in a cricket match. (2012)

The indigenous Vedda people of Sri Lanka should not play cricket, said cultural affairs minister T. B. Ekanayake, because it was detrimental to their culture, forcing them to wear shirts and trousers. Vedda linguist Uruwarige Wimalaratne replied that "Veddas have been playing cricket for a long time in their habitats, and our teachers coached us on the finer points of the game introduced by the colonial masters, but we never wore trousers or shoes." Vedda men used to wear only loincloths, but now normally wear sarongs. (2013)

Mark Carney, the Canadian who became governor of the Bank of England in 2013, has kept his promise to shake up the bank – by abolishing the annual cricket match. The game was traditionally the centrepiece of Governor's Day, the staff summer party; Carney's cricket-loving predecessor Lord King would captain his own Eleven, including celebrity players, against the Bank first team. A spokesman said: "The governor has not banned cricket. He wanted the activities at Governor's Day to be chosen by staff and their families. Staff chose a number of sports, such as rounders, football and tug-of-war." (2014)

A policeman in Lucknow has sent 1,000 rupees (about £10) to Indian captain Mahendra Singh Dhoni to thank him for leading the team to defeat in the World Cup semi-final. Amitabh Thakur, an inspector-general of civil defence, was grateful that Indians would not waste yet more working time watching the tournament. In an accompanying letter he told Dhoni: "It is your societal duty to not allow people to suspend government, financial and personal work in order to watch cricket matches." (2015)

FACEBOOKERS AND TWITS

The Australian Cricketers' Association says it has helped several leading players remove fake profiles from social networking sites. Ricky Ponting's manager, James Henderson, said he had closed down "three or four" bogus pages. The "I Laugh Hysterically Whenever Shane Watson Gets Dismissed in the 90s" page, allegedly posted by Ponting, was among the fakes. (2010)

Andrew Flintoff was criticised by disability campaigners and angry residents of Burnley after a series of Twitter messages crowing over the fact that Prince William and his future bride Kate Middleton visited both Blackburn and his home town, Preston – but not neighbouring Burnley. One tweet read: "The prince went to blackburn but drew the line at burnley, no 6 finger handshakes from the dingles for Wills". The six-finger reference is a local insult; the Dingles are an infamous clan in the downmarket TV soap *Emmerdale*. In response to complaints, Flintoff added that the Burnley town crier had been kept busy reading his tweets to the illiterates. "He doesn't even live in Preston, he moved away," responded the leader of Burnley council, Charlie Briggs. "He's not even a Preston fan, he supports a Manchester team." (2011)

Ireland's John Mooney, who hit the winning runs against England at the 2011 World Cup, was suspended after tweeting that he hoped Margaret Thatcher's death had been "slow and painful". Cricket Ireland chief executive Warren Deutrom called the comments "crass, insensitive and offensive". (2013)

The Derbyshire League has warned players about their use of social networks after a picture – described as "both pornographic and

defamatory" – was posted on Twitter making fun of new Premier League champions Swarkestone. (2013)

Kevin Pietersen had to be picked up by his wife after getting lost on a train following Surrey's Championship fixture with Essex. After leaving The Oval he boarded a train at Waterloo and excitedly tweeted: "Ferrari can't fly, so this is the quickest way to get home and beat London traffic". But the tweets grew increasingly desperate, and he eventually found himself in Wraysbury, eight miles from his home in Wentworth. "Never heard of the joint before – now I do!" he insisted on telling his almost three million followers. (2015)

Kevin Pietersen apologised on Twitter after making a joke about the fate of two suspected stowaways from Johannesburg who fell from a plane as it approached Heathrow. He sent a link to the story with the comment "Captain and opening bowler in England's WC cricket team in 2019 right there…" One of the two was killed, and the other critically injured. "Oh no…" began his next tweet. (2015)

Three Channel 9 commentators, Shane Warne, Kevin Pietersen and Michael Slater, have each been fined $A300 by Tasmanian police for failing to wear seatbelts. The three were recording a close-of-play update from a car and were issued with infringement notices after police reviewed a video posted on one of the trio's Facebook pages. (2016)

FAKE NEWS

Mohammed Isaq was banned for three years by the Quaid-e-Azam League in Yorkshire after sending in a fictitious score showing that his team Horton Print had beaten Bradford Shalima and thus won promotion; the game had actually been cancelled because they could not find a pitch. (1994)

The *Diss Express* newspaper in Norfolk published a "Wanted" poster offering a £10 reward for "the capture of a reckless villain" who sent the paper bogus reports involving the village team at Bressingham. Two of them were published, one of which claimed a local businessman had taken six wickets in an over. (1995)

Club cricketer Nadeem Alam, who reached the peak of his career playing for Huddersfield, posed as the former Pakistan Test player Nadeem Abbasi to give "expert" opinion on a succession of BBC radio programmes. The BBC announced an investigation. Alam said he had now given up his career as an Abbasi impersonator, but added: "I like to think I have been talking good cricket." The real Abbasi said: "If I ever find Nadeem Alam, I will punch him in the face for damaging the country's reputation." (2015)

Thirty-three aspirant cricketers, some of whom travelled long distances across India, were conned into turning up for nets in the hope of getting a place in the newly formed Rajkot IPL team. They had responded to messages on Facebook which instructed the boys to send sums of up to 3,000 rupees (£36) for the right to attend the trials. (2016)

After rumours of his death circulated on social media, the former Indian wicketkeeper Farokh Engineer denied them by issuing a message: "Friends, I am alive and kicking. I am very well and let me tell you I don't even need viagra at 78." (2016)

FAMOUS NAMES

The former England captain Brian Close, playing in a charity match for Norma Major's Eleven against the Bunburys, was caught one-handed in the gully by the former Rolling Stone Bill Wyman, who had a cigarette in his other hand. (1994)

Sir Donald Bradman has failed in an attempt to scrap a plan to rename the road from Adelaide Airport to the city Sir Donald Bradman Drive. The move became controversial when a cafe-owner decided to rename her business "Bradman's Cafe on the Drive", and then a sex shop applied to register the name "Erotica on Bradman". The mayor of West Torrens municipality, John Trainer, said he believed the sex shop's move was "the final straw" for the 92-year-old Don, who made a personal appeal to the council. Later, Australian prime minister John Howard added Bradman to a list of names – including those of the royal family – that cannot be exploited for commercial gain. (2000)

The first Steve Waugh Medal for the outstanding New South Wales player of the season was won by Steve Waugh. (2003)

Salil Ankola, the India Test-player-turned-actor, refused a film role that required him to play a cricketer who fixes matches. He said it was against his principles. (2003)

The Sri Lankan parliament broke standing orders to congratulate Muttiah Muralitharan on his marriage to Madhi Ramamurthy. No one had been congratulated on a wedding before. Speaker W. J. M. Lokubandra said: "Parliament has power to set a new example on occasions such as this as there are no two Muralitharans. Only one."(2005)

Andrew Flintoff revealed that on his wedding day in 2005 he had his favourite meal: fish fingers, chips and beans. "It was my day as well," he said. "Me and the kids' table, we had the same. Everyone else had confit chicken or something." (2005)

Indian wicketkeeper Mahendra Singh Dhoni spent five hours at the hairdressers in his home town of Ranchi having his hair straightened. Traffic snarled outside the salon when word spread that Dhoni was inside. (2006)

Twenty widely used Australian terms are to be incorporated into Microsoft Office's dictionary for use in Australia. The words can in future be used without being greeted by a squiggly red line. They include "sickie", "sheila", "dinki-di" and "Bradman". (2006)

Victoria Coverdale, 39, who runs a B&B west of Melbourne, has produced a book of 28 poems devoted to Shane Warne. She published them herself after being turned down even by a vanity publisher, who told her: "I've never known anything so singularly obsessive." The poems include "A Good Introduction", devoted to The Ball:
Mike Gatting's mouth became an O,
With a single delivery that changed the world,
Mike's, Shane's and mine, you know. (2006)

Shane Warne finished 96th out of 100 candidates in the annual poll to find the most trusted Australian – just ahead of convicted terrorism supporter David Hicks and controversial Muslim cleric Sheik Taj Din al-Hilali. Ricky Ponting was 29th. The winner was burns specialist Dr Fiona Wood. (2007)

Bookmakers Ladbrokes offered odds of 750 to 1 against Andrew Flintoff ever becoming a member of the Cabinet. "We think the only cabinet Freddie is likely to be in is the drinks cabinet," a spokesman said. (2007)

Mahendra Singh Dhoni has been given a fifteen-strong guard of policewomen in his home town of Ranchi to keep female fans away. This follows an incident in Calcutta when a girl broke through the security cordon and hugged him. (2008)

Andrew Flintoff won his planning battle to build a new mansion in a Cheshire village. Flintoff had to scale down his original plans for replacing the two-storey home he bought from the football manager Mark Hughes in 2007. But local councillors allowed him to build a new three-storey house which will include a swimming pool, a separate children's pool, a gym, sauna and steam room, cinema, bar, snooker and pool rooms and changing-rooms. The next-door neighbour, Carl Taylor, said the house would be unpleasant to look at. Flintoff also owns homes in Tenerife, Dubai, Barbados and London. (2008)

In Mahendra Singh Dhoni's home town of Ranchi, kitemaker Mohammad Talib said he was unable to meet demand from children wanting kites carrying the Indian captain's image: "Every day I prepare around 1,500 kites with photos of Dhoni. But I get over 2,000 young customers daily asking for them." (2009)

Olympic sprint champion Usain Bolt, a schoolboy cricket star, played in a charity match in Jamaica and hit West Indian captain Chris Gayle for a straight six. He also bowled Gayle, having welcomed him to the crease with a bouncer which brought the crowd at the Kaiser Sports Ground to its feet. "It's all coming back now," said Bolt. (2009)

Chris Hollins has become the third first-class cricketer to win the BBC's *Strictly Come Dancing* in the past five years, following Darren Gough and Mark Ramprakash. Hollins is best-known as a BBC sports reporter and the son of England footballer John Hollins. But he also scored 131 for Oxford in the 1994 University Match. (2009)

The Druid's Arms, Keighley, has been renamed the Dickie Bird in honour of the retired umpire. "I feel very proud," said Dickie. "I have had two racehorses named in my honour, and a fleet of taxis in India." (2011)

Australia's Transport Accident Commission defended their choice of Shane Warne to front a road-safety campaign less than a year after he was involved in a road-rage dispute with a cyclist. (2012)

The former England one-day captain Adam Hollioake, 40, achieved a draw on his debut as a mixed-martial-arts cage fighter in Queensland.

Hollioake said he loved every minute of his brawl with Joel Miller in front of a 1,500 crowd on the Gold Coast, though his wife Sherryn did not. After a bad first round, Hollioake outfought his opponent in the final two. He has been through many travails following the death of his brother Ben, including bankruptcy. He said of Sherryn: "She is a beautiful person and she wants me to follow my dreams. But I just think at the moment she wishes my dreams were something else." (2012)

Andrew Flintoff had an operation to repair a torn shoulder ligament after his first fight as a professional boxer. It was unclear whether the injury was sustained during his points victory over the American, Richard Dawson. Flintoff took a standing count in the second round, but held firm to win a narrow decision. The bout, much-hyped and much-criticised, looked, said *The Guardian*, "more like two burly farmhands trying to fend off a swarm of invisible bees than a boxing match." (2012)

Indian captain Mahendra Singh Dhoni successfully completed his first parachute jump as a "special" officer of the Indian territorial army's elite para regiment. However, some army officers have expressed disquiet at his involvement. "Army is spending money on Dhoni to train him as parachute," said one. "However, his knowledge and expertise are not going to be of any use to the Army or the nation." (2015)

Shane Warne has offered the theory that humans are descended from extra-terrestrials. He was musing with a fellow-contestant, dancer Bonnie Lythgoe, while in the Kruger National Park on the Australian version of *I'm a Celebrity…Get Me Out of Here!*, and wondering why the local monkeys had not evolved into humans… "Because, I'm saying, aliens. We started from aliens." (2016)

The former West Indian player Tino Best said in his autobiography that he had slept with "between 500 and 650" women. "I reckon I'm the best-looking bald guy in the world," he explained. (2016)

Sir Ian Botham, in his role as a shooting enthusiast, clashed with BBC wildlife presenter Chris Packham on the Radio 4 *Today* programme on the day the grouse-shooting season began, the "Inglorious Twelfth" as Packham called it. "It's the gamekeepers who look after the moors," said

Botham, who is the figurehead for a campaign group called You Forgot the Birds. "It's only people like Chris that want to sabotage nature by banning success." Packham said grouse moors were ecologically damaged and that endangered birds of prey were being killed by game-keepers to keep grouse numbers high. (2016)

Andrew Flintoff opened to polite but mixed reviews when *Fat Friends – The Musical*, an adaptation of a TV show about slimming, opened at the Leeds Grand Theatre prior to a national tour. Lancastrian Flintoff played "nice-but-dim" Kevin, fiancé of the bride desperate to fit into her wedding dress, in a story set in the unLancastrian suburb of Headingley. Flintoff "proves he can do more than play cricket", said the *Yorkshire Post*. He captured Kevin well and won plenty of laughs, according to the *Huddersfield Daily Examiner*, "but sadly his vocals just weren't up to the task". *The Press*, York, praised his "warm-toned" singing but said his movement was "not exactly comfortable". (2017)

Andrew Flintoff says he believes the world is flat, and is considering a trip to the Flat Earth International Conference in the US in 2018. Speaking on his own BBC podcast, he asked "If you're in a helicopter and you hover, why does the Earth not come to you if it's round? Why, if we're hurtling through space, why would water stay still? Why is it not wobbling?" (2017)

... NOT FAMOUS ENOUGH

The Gujarat government refused to allow Indian wicketkeeper Parthiv Patel and fast bowler Irfan Pathan to defer their 12th-standard exams after they were selected for the tour of Pakistan. "A lot of other students may queue up citing various reasons," said a spokesman. (2004)

Pakistan off-spinner Arshad Khan was ordered by his employers, Allied Bank, to leave the squad for the one-day series against India and return to banking duties. An official told Arshad that the Pakistan Cricket Board's request for his release "could not meet approval of competent authority". (2006)

The family of Mushtaq Ali, India's first Test match centurion who died in 2005, were found living in a cramped, derelict house in Indore because their father was never able to move into a modern bungalow allotted to him by the state government. When the family tried to get the keys in 1995, they found a judge living there and he never moved out, Mushtaq's son Gulrez said. (2006)

Residents of the picturesque village of Castle Combe were less than enthused by the arrival in their midst of Kevin Pietersen and Liberty X singer Jessica Taylor, who married in the church there. Locals wanting to lay flowers on graves in the churchyard found the way blocked by bouncers. Reports that villagers had hung lights from their windows to create a winter wonderland for the couple were dismissed as "complete rubbish" by Adrian Bishop, vice-chairman of the parish council. He said the only lights were at the £300-a-night hotel that was completely booked out by the wedding party, which included several of Pietersen's England team-mates. Darren Gough was best man. (2007)

Rock star Alice Cooper, 65, visited the *Test Match Special* box at Lord's during the South Africa Test. On being introduced to "Alice", Geoff Boycott shook hands with Cooper's wife. (2012)

GOD AMONG MEN

An 18-year-old girl committed suicide in Mysore, India after being told that her hero Sachin Tendulkar might have to retire because of back trouble. She poured paraffin over herself then set herself alight. (1999)

The Indian government waived customs duty and the requirements for a roadworthiness certificate so Sachin Tendulkar could import a £90,000 Ferrari Modena 360. Bharat Petroleum also blended special fuel so the car could run on Indian roads; the 97-octane petrol the car requires is not sold in India. (2004)

Tendulkar has sold his image rights to Iconix, a subsidiary of the advertising agency Saatchi & Saatchi, for £22 million in a three-year deal. (2006)

Tendulkar is India's highest earner, according to a new survey, making 1,163 rupees (more than £13) every minute, compared to 361 rupees for film star Amitabh Bachcan and 57 paise (0.6p) for the prime minister, Manmohan Singh. (2006)

Tendulkar is to appear in comic books as the Master-Blaster, a superhero. (2007)

Tendulkar lookalike Balvir Chand pleaded for help after his planned twenty-day tour of India to coincide with the World Cup was ruined by India's exit: "Sachin allowed me to lead a respectable life but today I am jobless and homeless." Travel company boss Joe Rajan offered to pay Chand's rent. Thanking Rajan, Chand said he was sorry that his "god", Sachin, had not responded to the appeal. (2007)

A new variety of mango, developed by a horticulturist in Uttar Pradesh, has been named "Sachin". However, the grower claimed he would not be selling the fruit. "Our Sachin is a world hero and he is priceless," said Hajj Kalimullah. "My attempt will be to send all the mangoes on this tree to Sachin so he can enjoy them with his friends." (2010)

A de luxe edition of Tendulkar's autobiography is to be published in 2011, in which the signature page will be tinted with a sample of the author's blood. The 852-page "blood edition" of the *Official Sachin Tendulkar Opus* will weigh 37kg and cost about £50,000. Only ten copies are being printed and all have been pre-ordered. Publisher Karl Fowler admitted: "It's not to everyone's taste and some may think it's a bit weird. But the key thing here is that Sachin Tendulkar to millions of people is a religious icon. And we thought how, in a publishing form, can you get as close to your god as possible?" Tendulkar later denied the blood-letting. (2010)

Tendulkar was made an honorary group captain in the Indian Air Force, complete with uniform and epaulettes, at a ceremony in New Delhi. (2010)

An Indian tax tribunal upheld an appeal from Tendulkar that he should be classed as an actor for his modelling work. This enabled him to claim tax deductions. "As a model, the assessee brings to his work a degree of imagination, creativity and skill to arrange elements in a manner that would affect human senses and emotions and to have an aesthetic value," the tribunal ruled. (2011)

Cricket Australia flew a cup to mark Tendulkar's 100th international hundred to every venue where he played in Australia in 2011–12, awaiting the moment for presentation, which never came. (2012)

The Mumbai Cricket Association intends to shower Tendulkar with a hundred gold coins for reaching 100 international centuries. (2012)

A painting depicting the highlights of Tendulkar's career, by the British-based artist Sacha Jafri, has been sold for $750,000. The proceeds will go to the M. S. Dhoni Foundation to support poor children. (2012)

Ratilal Parmar, 56, whose hobby is collecting banknotes that have special associations with Tendulkar, has acquired a new prize: a ten-rupee note numbered 240412, the date of Tendulkar's 39th birthday. Parmar hoped to present his hero with the notes connected with his milestones, especially 160312, the date of the 100th international hundred. He estimated that he had spent a million rupees building his collection, sometimes pleading with bank clerks for help. (2012)

Tendulkar has been sworn in as a member of the Indian upper house, the Rajya Sabha. "It has been my dream to be remembered as someone who worked for all sports instead of just cricket statistics," he said after taking the oath. However, he warned that, as an active player, he would continue to focus on his own game. Tendulkar was chosen as one of the twelve members of the parliament the president is allowed to nominate, although some critics claimed that a sportsman did not fulfil the criterion of "special knowledge or practical experience in… literature, science, art and social service" specified for selection under the constitution. (2012) *See also page 88.*

Australian prime minister Julia Gillard made Tendulkar an honorary member of the Order of Australia on a visit to India, but the award came under fire for not meeting the rule that such awards for non-Australians should reflect "extraordinary service to Australia or humanity at large". Independent MP Rob Oakeshott said: "I love Sachin, I love cricket, but I just have a problem with soft diplomacy. It's about the integrity of the honours list." (2012)

Tendulkar has been listed as a casual labourer in Goa and eligible for relief under a government scheme to help rural workers. This is thought to be a scam perpetrated by officials rather than a coincidence, since other applicants' names include Kapil Dev, Sourav Ganguly and Ricky Ponting. (2014)

Tendulkar sparked a Pietersenesque social-media frenzy when he had dinner in an Oxfordshire village after watching Andy Murray at Wimbledon. He posted pictures of himself by a bus stop with the words "In Great Haseley, Oxfordshire. Missed the last bus, can anyone give me a lift?" He was bombarded with messages from adoring fans either offering to help or apologising that they couldn't – mainly because they were in India. One claimed to have arrived to look for him. Tendulkar was indeed in Great Haseley, but had travelled by car. Two days later, he reposted the same pictures, overwritten with the words: "Not the bus. But some seem to have missed the joke." One respondent said: "God-level sarcasm is obviously difficult to understand for humans." (2015)

The 1,895 residents of a remote village in Andhra Pradesh have had their lives transformed since they were "adopted" by Tendulkar a year ago under a national scheme whereby MPs and VIPs help a poor village. The Ministry of Rural Development named the village, Puttamrajuvari Kandriga, among the top three villages of the three hundred involved as an example of what can be done. The villagers have gained paved roads, footpaths, drainage, power, drinking water, sanitation, a hall, a school and a sports ground. (2015)

… AND A FEW UNBELIEVERS

The scoresheet for the 664-run schoolboy partnership between Sachin Tendulkar and Vinod Kambli in 1988 has been destroyed by the Mumbai School Sports Association. "It was like any other sheet from a normal game, and a few years back, white ants ate into those sheets," said the association secretary H. S. Bhor. "The scoresheet was kept along with all the other records of games and has since been incinerated as we could not store them all. You cannot expect us to store files that are twenty-five years old." (2013)

Politicians criticised Tendulkar for his attendance record in the Rajya Sabha, the Indian upper house, an unelected body to which he was appointed in 2012. Tendulkar was said to have attended only three times in 2013, not at all so far in 2014, and never to have taken part in a debate. There were demands for him to stand down. "Why have you chosen to become a member of parliament if you don't attend?" asked Congress member Rajeev Shukla. Tendulkar later requested leave of absence because his brother was undergoing heart surgery. This was granted, despite opposition. One member, Naresh Agarwal, said the house was unanimous that Tendulkar had no respect for it. (2014)

After Sachin Tendulkar complained to British Airways about poor service and what he called a "don't care" attitude from staff, the airline responded by apologising – and asking for his full name and address. This enraged Tendulkar's fan army, who declared social-media war on the airline for not recognising him. Some called for the Indian prime minister to cancel his visit to the UK. Other posts included: "How dare you ask his full name, you swines," and, more subtly, "Try Sachin Ramesh Tendulkar, India. I'm sure this is enough." (2015)

GONE MISSING

Detective John Bavister spotted his wife's stolen car while waiting to bat for Whittlesey Second Eleven at Crowland, Lincolnshire. His captain dropped him down the order to give him time to arrest two youths. (1995)

Robin Wightman was recorded in the scorebook as being "absent huffed" when he failed to bat for Whiteleas against East Rainton in the North-East Durham League. Wightman had stormed off the pitch when his captain refused to let him bowl the last over, even though he had taken seven wickets. Then he went home. MCC assistant secretary John Jameson said the notation was quite legitimate and should count as a dismissal in the averages, as with "timed out". (1995)

A batsman called Cordingly was recorded as "absent babysitting" in the match between Cliffe and Yalding in Kent. (1996)

Winslow Town from Buckinghamshire turned up to fulfil a fixture at Kempston, Bedfordshire, and began playing the wrong team at the wrong ground. They were supposed to be playing Kempston Ramblers but found themselves playing Kempston Meltis, whose own opponents had failed to turn up. No one realised the mistake until a Ramblers player came looking for the Winslow team, and they were led off to play the right game. "I have played against Ramblers a number of times over the years and I thought all their batsmen must have retired or died off," said Winslow batsman Ron Phillips. (1996)

Cliff Spinks, batting for Langleybury, Hertfordshire, in a cup-tie against Northwood, decided he had had enough after scoring 31 not out and threw his bat at the stumps. The fielders' appeals were turned down under Law 35, because he had not been playing the ball or attempting a

run. Spinks then appealed himself and, when this was rejected, walked off. He was given "retired out" and said: "I have been playing too much cricket." (1996)

A fielder who chased a ball hit out of the ground down a steep hill brought it back by bus. Paul Crabb, playing for Ilfracombe Rugby Club in Devon against Woolacombe, caught up with the ball a quarter of a mile from the ground at Hele. When he saw the bus coming, he decided to hop on it. The driver was sporting enough to overlook the fact that he did not have the 46p for his fare. (1996)

When Gareth Lewis struck a six during a Scarborough Beckett League game at Nawton Grange, the ball landed on a car radiator grille, continued up the A170, and wound up in a garage in Kirkbymoorside, three and a half miles away. (2003)

Agencies are sprouting in India offering would-be migrants illegal entry to the UK via cricket tours. Five members of a women's side from

Jalandhar, northern India, recently disappeared when supposedly playing in a tournament in Herefordshire. "We will attach you to a cricket club," one agent assured an undercover reporter. "All you need to do is slip out of the team once you land in the UK. Though I cannot assure you a job there, I have contacts among lawyers who can help."(2003)

Staxton Second Eleven were handed the Scarborough Beckett League's Division D title when their rivals Grindale were unable to raise a team for the crucial match. Their players were busy harvesting. (2008)

Children in Abbottabad, the town in Pakistan where US forces found and killed Osama bin Laden, said they often hit cricket balls over the twenty-foot walls guarding the bin Laden compound. However, they were always told there was no ball there and given money instead. (2011)

One of the most bizarre games in the history of the Kent League got under way when only five players from Hythe (top of the table) arrived for the start of their match at Holmesdale (bottom). However, Holmesdale captain Mark Epps insisted on starting. "We play hard, but we play by the rules," he said. Epps also refused to let various family members field as subs, saying they were not registered. The five kept the score down to 165 for two after 25 overs, when the other six, held up on the M20, arrived. None of them was allowed to bowl, however, because they had not been on the field long enough. Even so, Hythe, facing 340, got a draw. "The spirit of cricket was totally absent," said stand-in Hythe captain James Watson. "To get a draw is a top, top result." (2011)

A vicar has been reunited with the cricket ball he lost as a seven-year-old – thirty-eight years earlier. Rev. Simon Ward grew up in the rectory at Belton, Norfolk, and when the family moved out he jokingly asked the new occupants to look out for the ball. It resurfaced when work was being done on a pond. 'It was brand new, a nice shiny cricket ball, my first one," said Ward. "We barely got the first over finished before it got lost, I remember I cried my eyes out. It's now a shrivelled husk of its former glory, not the red shiny ball I fell in love with. But it was charming to discover it." (2017)

HAPPY HITTERS

Rob Kelly, 24, a sausage factory worker from Chard, hit 11 sixes off consecutive balls for Buckland St Mary against Taunton Casuals in Division Three of the West Somerset League. (1993)

Shaheed Ramzan, 25, hit 113 not out in 25 minutes at Maidenhead, Berkshire, then apologised to opponents and drove off to a family wedding. (1993)

Corey Hojnacki, 19, scored 426 out of a total of 710 for Heinz Southern Districts against Silverton in the Dandenong & District Association C grade, adding 338 on the second Saturday to the 88 he scored a week earlier. He hit 31 sixes and 36 fours. Hojnacki's own bat had been stolen and he used his father's old "Austral" bat. "It's as thick as a tree trunk," Hojnacki said. "I only had to block and the ball went for four." (1994)

Stuart Hensman of the Redback Cricket Club in Sydney went in to bat, having told team-mates he would have to retire after half an hour because of an urgent appointment. He was late for the appointment, but only just, after scoring 140 from 56 balls. (1997)

Adryan Winnan, an England Under-18 rugby player, was anxious to nurse a calf injury and not run too much in a Cornish League match for Penryn against Wendron. So his 300 not out included 15 sixes and 24 fours. (2000)

Spencer Chorlton, playing for Yoxford against Mallards in Suffolk, hit seven sixes in an over that included a no-ball. Chorlton, the 17-year-old captain of Framlingham College, raced from 50 to 100 in 14 balls. (2002)

Simon Williams hit 40 and 28 in consecutive overs from the same (unnamed) bowler – the 40 comprised six sixes plus a four off a no-ball. Williams, who scored 100, was playing for Werribee South against Wyndhamvale in the Williamstown & District competition, Victoria. (2003)

Jonathan Hughes made 42 in an over playing for North Leeds against Hall Park in a cup-tie. Medium-pacer Craig Hobson bowled two no-balls and Hughes hit six sixes, a four and a two. "It seemed to take for ever because of the time spent looking for the ball," Hughes said. (2006)

Australian Damian Cialini hit 303 not out in a 45-over match for Yoxford against Easton in the Suffolk Premier League. Cialini said he did not know he had scored a triple-century. "I'd lost count. I thought I was being clapped for my 250." (2006)

Rob Ellis of Glasshouses struck eight sixes in an eight-ball over from left-arm spinner Tim Hendry in a Harrogate & District evening knockout match against Blubberhouses. Ellis, 19, finished with 138 not out. His team-mate Ian Sunderland described the performance as "absolutely amazing" but admitted: "I missed the last five sixes because I was too busy fishing the first three balls out of the River Nidd." (2006)

Jack Robertson of Eltham College Under-15s scored 44 in an over against Colfe's – four sixes and five fours. It was a ten-ball over containing four no-balls. Robertson plays for the college first team and has ambitions to play professionally. "I guess I just hit the first few and it seemed like fun, and just continued to try and hit the ball as far as possible, he said. "I don't think I'll ever get the chance to do this again." (2009)

In Sussex, Marc Livesley hit nine successive sixes for Kings Arms, Billingshurst, in a cup-tie against Cherry Tree, and reached a century off 32 balls. (2010)

Jack Lane, 16, hit seven sixes in an over playing for John Hampden Grammar School, High Wycombe, against Reading Blue Coat School. Six, one of them off a no-ball, went over the short leg-side boundary before Lane hit the last ball back over the bowler's head. (2011)

Coming in at 30 for four, Shane Basile was next man out at 190, having scored 126 from 27 balls. Playing for Coomera-Hope Island against Burleigh Heads in a sixth-grade match in Queensland, Basile butchered his century from 21 deliveries. He hit six sixes off his first seven balls and later six sixes in an over. Cricket Gold Coast later ordered Basile to move up a grade. (2013)

South African Shawn Dyson hit 40 off an over for Wath against Conisborough in the South Yorkshire Senior League. He struck sixes off the first six balls, one of them a no-ball – and the seventh fell just inches short. He finished with an unbeaten 151 from 68 balls. (2016)

Delhi cricketer Mohit Ahlawat, 21, scored 300 not out in a local Twenty20 match for Maavi against Friends. The runs came off 72 balls with 39 sixes and 14 fours. Ahlawat had failed to score in his last three first-class innings. That night he got a call from the Delhi Daredevils. (2017)

Josh Dunstan scored 307 with 40 sixes for West Augusta in a 35-over match against Central Stirling in Port Augusta, South Australia. Dunstan made his runs out of a total of 354, and 318 while he was at the crease. He shared a seventh-wicket stand of 203 with Ben Russell, who contributed just five. (2017)

On his 20th birthday Shane Dadswell scored 490 off 151 balls playing for North-West University in Potchefstroom against Potch Dorp Cricket Club. Dadswell hit 57 sixes and 27 fours. The team made 677 for three off 50 overs and won by 387 runs. The previous week Dadswell had scored 126 off 38 balls. He said he was "a bit of an attacking batsman". (2017)

... NOT SO HAPPY

An elderly woman pushing her bicycle past the ground at Burghill, Herefordshire, was taken to hospital after being hit by a six in a game against Hay-on-Wye. "It was certainly very unlucky," said the Burghill club chairman Len Sparrow, "especially as the lad who hit it normally can't play leg-side." (1993)

Sharon Scott of Kington, Herefordshire, was taken to hospital for observation after being hit on the head by a six struck by her husband, Clive

(who played in the 1993 village final at Lord's), while she was wheeling their baby round the boundary. "She probably cost me a century," Clive said. "I went into my shell for a while after that." (1994)

Graeme Parkinson, 33, hit a six through his parents' windscreen as they sat and watched him from their car in Darwen, Lancashire. (1995)

Craig Scully won the last match of the season for Chipping Sodbury in Gloucestershire with a six that broke his car windscreen. (1996)

Neil Carey, 24, from Bath, failed to get a batting average after scoring 531 runs in the season for St Stephen's without being dismissed. (1998)

Sussex dentist Rob Hemingway, playing for St Peters against Horsted Keynes in April, became perhaps the first batsman of 1999 to hit a six through his own car windscreen. "It was quite nice to connect with the ball so early in the season," he said, "but then I heard the crack and thought, oops, whose car is that?" (1999)

Umer Rashid was scoring freely for Richmondshire against Darlington RA in the North Yorkshire & South Durham League when bowler Stewart Morgan asked the umpire to measure his bat. It was found to be a quarter of an inch wider than the permitted 4¼ inches. Rashid said he had bought the bat in Pakistan and had no idea it was illegal; the league took no action. (1999)

Playing for Chester-le-Street Under-13s against Eppleton, Anthony McMahon hit six sixes in an over, but still finished on the losing side. (2003)

Former BBC newsreader Angela Rippon's tenure as president of the Lady Taverners got off to an inauspicious start: there was no sign of her when she was asked to say a few words at the start of a celebrity match on the Lord's Nursery Ground. She had dashed off to get her car windscreen repaired after it was smashed by a ball. (2011)

Thirteen-year-old Bhupen Lalwani of Don Bosco School, Matunga, became the latest addition to the list of players who have made extreme scores in Mumbai's annual Giles Shield. Lalwani scored 398 out of 715 for five against IES Modern English School (Dadar), who lost by an innings and 590. He said "it hurt" to miss a quadruple-century. (2012)

The chief executive of Hawke's Bay Cricket Association, Craig Findlay, scored 307 from 115 balls against a team of schoolboys aged 15 and 16 – and was bombarded with complaints. The St John's College captain asked Findlay, who played first-class cricket for Central Districts, several times if he might retire, but he said only that he would think about it. "That CEO should be nurturing these players, not trying to show off and have his score on the back page," said one of many messages to the local paper. Findlay was believed to have been making a point, since he thought the school should not be competing in the senior men's grade. He seemed unrepentant: "To create champions you have to be tough." (2014)

HEROICS (SERIOUSLY)

The England bowler Phil DeFreitas was praised for saving the life of an elderly neighbour at Bretby, Derbyshire, whose kitchen caught fire. DeFreitas climbed through a window and, when he found 85-year-old Ted Graham asleep in the smoke-filled room, carried him to safety. (1994)

One-armed all-rounder Dan Holder from Cheltenham was picked for Gloucestershire Under-16s in response to his form at school and club level. He was born with a stump on his left arm but hits hard, bowls fast and fields tidily. "My arm is as strong as two, really," he said, "because I've used it for everything all my life." (1999)

Garry Cook, 47, of Abingdon, Oxfordshire, scored the first century of his career three months after a quadruple heart-bypass operation. (1999)

Colin Moir hobbled off on 56 not out while batting for Stoneywood/Dyce Second Eleven in Aberdeenshire, telling bewildered Methlick fielders he had broken his leg. Not all of them realised it was his artificial leg. He took his spare out of his car boot, and returned to finish on an unbeaten 71 with a six off the last ball. (2008)

Probably the only medal awarded for bravery on the cricket field was sold at auction for £21,600 yesterday. The George Cross was awarded to Major Douglas Brett of the Indian Army when Hindu protesters attacked a match in Chittagong in 1934. Major Brett saved spectators and fellow players from a rebel brandishing a revolver. He died in 1963. (2010)

An 11-year-old boy born with no hands or forearms has been displaying remarkable cricketing gifts. Kearan Tongue-Gibbs, from Redditch, Worcestershire, is a spinner who grips the ball in the fold of his arm. He is playing alongside able-bodied children at school and at Astwood Bank Cricket Club. Kearan is "really talented", said Mike Harris of Astwood Bank. "To get the accuracy is something I can't really understand how he does." (2011)

Jif Wilkins from Wiltshire village club Goatacre had to be carried to the crease to hit the runs that not merely won the game but got the team promoted to the West of England Premier League. Wilkins had injured his knee fielding in a crucial match against Cheltenham and was unable to move. But he refused an ambulance "in case it goes down to the wire and I have to bat". It did, and he did. He whacked his first ball past cover for four then worked another away for his runner to scramble the single that tied the scores and secured the promotion place which would otherwise have gone to Cheltenham. He then hit the winning four for good measure. Goatacre captain Ed Wilkins said: "I don't like to praise him too much as he's my brother but it was a great effort." (2017)

KIT AND CABOODLE

Eddie Bancroft, a seam bowler with size 16 feet who plays for Churchtown, Lancashire, received a £260 grant from the Foundation for Sport and the Arts to buy handmade boots. (1993)

New Earswick Cricket Club in Yorkshire paid £105 for a £10,000 carpet with the letters NCC woven into it. The carpet became a symbol of bureaucratic waste when a government agency threw it out after only three years because the Funding Agency for Schools had taken over from the National Curriculum Council. "The lettering is near enough," said club trustee Geoff Clarkson, "and it also happens to match our colour scheme." (1994)

A London insurance broker paid £6,000 at a benefit auction for a short-sleeved shirt said to have been worn by Brian Lara during his innings of 375 against England. Tipped off by a friend, he later watched the video and discovered that Lara wore a long-sleeved shirt throughout. (1994)

The Thames Valley League banned Marlow's new strip, which had a gold top, a blue band and their sponsors' name across the back. "It's a head in the sand attitude," said club secretary Alan Tierney. (1998)

The Huddersfield League banned Kexborough Cricket Club from wearing new shirts which had their names and squad numbers on the back. "Cricketers should be attired as if they are playing in a real Test match," said league chairman Roger France. "We are not a Test side," said Kexborough secretary Neil Hinchcliffe. "We are Kexborough." (2005)

Bristol teenager Freddie Owsley found a stick among rocks on the beach at Polzeath, Cornwall, and decided it would make a useful bat for a game of beach cricket. It was only after playing for a while that a family friend, a doctor, concluded this was no ordinary bat. Archaeologists later confirmed it was a human femur, probably from a sailor whose body had been washed ashore before 1808 – when a law was passed saying such remains should be buried in consecrated ground. (2011)

Karl Lagerfeld, creative director of the fashion house Chanel, unveiled his "Cruise 2014" collection in Singapore. This included – as well as cocktail dresses with lace, shimmering sequins and ruffles – "sporty cricket whites complete with ribbed V-neck jumpers, boyish shirts, leg pads and cricket bats". (2013)

Five senior lawyers, including a High Court judge, were denied admission to the Madras Cricket Club for wearing traditional dhotis. They were invited to attend the launch of a legal book rather than a cricketing function, and the judge, Justice D. Hariparanthaman, said there was no mention of a dress code on the invitation. The club president (and chairman of the International Cricket Council) N. Srinivasan promised a change of rule after the chief minister of Tamil Nadu, Jayalalithaa Jayaram, threatened state action and called it "sartorial despotism". (2014)

LONG HAULS

Former New Zealand wicketkeeper Adam Parore, 40, reached the summit of Mount Everest in an attempt to raise £50,000 for charity. He described himself as "buggered", having shown signs of hypoxia, a potentially fatal shortage of oxygen. "I spent about twenty minutes to half an hour up there," Parore said. "I had great plans on what I should do and how I might feel, but in the end it was a bit of an anticlimax. I just wanted to get down and live." (2011)

Former Somerset batsman Ricky Bartlett has raised $NZ50,000 for charity after spending a year playing all 419 golf courses in New Zealand. He covered 7,542 holes and hit 31,594 shots – but his handicap actually went up. (2007)

Jason Rawson, 39, who plays for Salesbury near Blackburn, claimed a record for the longest run-up in history after running a pre-season marathon concluding with a formal 1.6-mile run-in – starting at the Shajan Indian restaurant on the A59 – to bowl to a batsman waiting in position on the club ground. Ian Riley scrambled a leg-bye. The stunt raised £3,250 for club funds. (2010)

Blunham Cricket Club, in Bedfordshire, have reclaimed the currently much sought-after record for the world's longest cricket match. Blunham's first and second teams played through 105 consecutive hours, many of them windy and rainy, to recapture the record from Cornwall Cricket Club in New Zealand. Blunham set a mark of 59 hours in 2008, which was then beaten twice. The latest marathon raised £17,000 for the club and charities. (2010)

The record for the longest continuous match has been broken again, this time by Loughborough University staff, who battled atrocious weather

for 150 hours 20 minutes. One substitute fielder was allowed per side. "We had torrential rain and hailstones the size of golf balls but, in true British tradition, we kept calm and carried on," said organiser Chris Hughes. (2012) *This actually comprised 19 separate but continuous matches, and was still recognised in June 2018 by Guinness World Records as the longest cricket-playing marathon.*

The Worsley Cup quarter-final between East Lancashire and Enfield, supposedly a one-day game, stretched for more than a month owing to continual rain. East Lancashire captain Ockert Erasmus finally settled the game by 11 runs with a hat-trick on July 12, just when Enfield appeared to be heading for victory, thirty-three days after the match should have started. This was the twelfth scheduled day and the fifth actual playing day of a match staged on two different grounds – along the way it was switched to Enfield, which was slightly drier. The Warwickshire all-rounder Keith Barker began the game playing for his home club Enfield and took an early catch but, when it rained after four overs, had to leave – and could not be replaced. (2012)

The record for the longest net batting session has been claimed and re-claimed several times since 2012. Such efforts have been regularly recorded in

Chronicle: by Jade Child of Tasmania (2012), Alby Shale from Oxfordshire (2013), whose net bowlers included then prime minister David Cameron, and then Dave Newman and Richard Wells from Billingborough, Lincolnshire (2014). According to Guinness the next entry stood as the record at the start of 2018:

The improbable but evidently much-coveted record for the longest individual net session was broken again when Virag Mare of Pune batted for 50 hours, five minutes and 51 seconds, beating the previous best of 48 hours. He faced 14,682 balls. (2015)

Rwanda's national team captain Eric Dusingizimana was reported to have batted for 51 hours (including the permitted five-minute hourly breaks) in the capital, Kigali. His bowlers included Tony Blair, who happened to be passing. The aim was to raise awareness of Rwandan cricket and to raise money for a stadium. (2016) *This had not, in June 2018, been recognised as a record by Guinness.*

LOST IN TRANSLATION

Derbyshire County Cricket Club's advert for a new secretary produced 125 replies, mostly from applicants who listed their typing and shorthand speeds. (1996)

Philip Halden, a British businessman kidnapped in Colombia and held in the jungle by guerrillas for eight months, taught his captors cricket after carving a bat and wooden balls with a machete. But he said both his kidnappers and his fellow hostages preferred playing soccer and, when the bat broke, he was not encouraged to carve another one. (1996)

The Easington Primary Care Trust in County Durham is compiling a dialect guide for doctors new to the region so they can understand which part of their patients' bodies might be aching. Among the examples of useful words given by the Trust was "warne", meaning belly. (2006)

US soldiers who invaded Grenada in 1983 were advised by British diplomats to learn cricket, according to a document released by the UK government. Britain thought the American forces were behaving insensitively, and advised that they could win local support by "mending roads, painting churches, giving children's parties and being photographed doing so. They could even have a shot at playing cricket. Let the Grenadians teach them something". (2013)

MARCHING ON THEIR STOMACHS

In keeping with a tradition dating back to Don Bradman's time, the Australian captain Allan Border was presented with a whortleberry pie by the Castle Hotel, Taunton. Unfortunately, the whortleberry was out of season on the Quantocks and the tradition was maintained only when a local man came up with a supply from his freezer. (1993)

The village team from Stoke Canon, Devon, has disbanded after other teams refused to play them because of the quality of their teas. The club had failed to replace their regular tea-maker, Vi Dolling, after she retired in 1993. Younger wives and girlfriends were less keen, and the men were forced to make the teas themselves. "Some of the players made really terrible sandwiches," said the captain Tim Keehner. "Our teas became notorious." (1999)

Minor Counties umpire Steve Kuhlmann, in Torquay to take charge of the game between Devon and Berkshire, was kicked out of his hotel after asking for fresh fruit instead of a cooked breakfast. (2005)

An 80-year family tradition at Oulton Park Cricket Club, Cheshire, has ended after the retirement of tea-lady Margaret Parker, 91. Her brother-in-law, a local shopkeeper, took on the task in 1926 after Oulton Hall, the stately home whose staff had previously provided the cricket teas, burned down. (2006)

The Saddleworth & District League's annual meeting voted to abolish players' teas at league matches – although the decision was declared void by the committee on a technicality. The meeting also wanted to cut the

interval to fifteen minutes. Clubs in the North Manchester area said they were struggling to find volunteers. Opponents said they should call in outside caterers. (2007)

A pint of beer at the Harare Sports Club cricket ground now costs 800 million Zimbabwean dollars, about 80p on the black market. (2008)

Hazel Smith of Melbourne has been awarded the ICC Centenary Volunteer Medal after providing sandwiches and scones to cricketers over the past sixty-eight years. Mrs Smith, 88, has made the teas at the Cameron Cricket Club since she married and gave up playing herself when she was 20. (2009)

Retired teachers Carole and Mike Russell, both in their seventies, were denied admission to the Lancashire–Glamorgan match in Colwyn Bay because they were carrying metal spoons to eat strawberries. The steward also objected to their jars containing tea and coffee. The club blamed "over-enthusiastic" stewarding, but said their ban on metal cutlery would continue. "What do you think two pensioners are going to do with a couple of dessert spoons?" asked Carole. (2010)

Winners of the annual tournament in Jawhar, Maharashtra, were given edible prizes instead of the customary money. The winning team won a goat, the runners-up five cockerels, and every boundary-hitter got a boiled egg. "In the past we have experienced allegations of rigging and fights over prize money. This time, all willingly shared their prizes," said local coach Umesh Tamore. (2017)

MEN OF GOD

A vicar who swore and bowled roast potatoes at fellow guests while speaking at the Minehead club dinner was pardoned by his bishop after apologising for having "one drink too many". Rev. Richard Allen, vicar of Williton, Somerset, was finally led from the room after spilling coffee into the club president's lap. "I may be a vicar," he said, "but I am an ordinary man." (1994)

The Bishop of Ludlow, the Right Reverend John Saxbee, has started wearing a baseball cap fitted with radio and earplugs so he can keep in touch with the Test score. "At a recent meeting of rural deans, I was

obliged to wear the cap throughout to keep everyone informed," he said. (1995)

The Bishop of Durham announced his decision to retire live on *Test Match Special*. The Right Rev. Michael Turnbull said, while a guest on the programme: "I have long had an ambition to announce my retirement on *Test Match Special*. And that is precisely what I am doing." (2002)

More than seven hundred people attended a Twenty20 match at Grace Road between Christian clergy and Muslim imams to mark the fifth anniversary of the September 11 attacks. "The atmosphere was really great," said the Leicester diocesan inter-faith adviser, Dr Andrew Wingate. "Each group clapped each other at the end." The imams won by 27 runs, repeating their victory at football earlier in the year. The umpires were Jewish and Hindu. (2006)

An 84-year-old vicar was formally allowed back in to Kimberley Institute Cricket Club in Nottingham seventy years after being banned from the ground. As a 14-year-old schoolboy, the not-then-Reverend Dennis Hibbert was thrown out and told never to return for calling a fielder "a big fat fool" when he let the ball between his legs. He has now been officially readmitted. "I've been purged of my sins," he said. "My family think it's a hoot." (2008)

Jesus may have played a version of cricket, according to a scholar's interpretation of an ancient Armenian manuscript. Professor Abraham Terian said that a passage in the Armenian Gospel of the Infancy, dating from the sixth century AD, refers to the young Jesus walking on the waters of the Sea of Galilee while playing with a stick and ball. (2008)

Michael Claughton offered to umpire the goodwill match between the Church of England and the Vatican at Canterbury, but was turned down because his great-great-grandfather was a bishop. Claughton, 65, has eighteen years' experience as a league umpire in Kent. Paul Handley, editor of the *Church Times*, which organised the match, said the umpires should be "theologically neutral". (2014)

MISFORTUNES

At least ten children were treated at hospital in Chilaw, Sri Lanka, for eye injuries as cricket fever gripped the country after the national team's World Cup win. A doctor said cricket was being played on every available open space, often with pebbles or stones instead of a ball. Onlookers, mainly small children, were inevitable casualties, he said. (1996)

Wicketkeeper Gavin Roebuck, of Darfield in the Barnsley Sunday League, had his elbow broken by team-mates congratulating him on securing a match-winning stumping. (1996)

Groundsman Brian Lucas had his false teeth crushed by his roller at the Perkins Cricket Club in Shropshire. They shot out of his mouth when he sneezed. (1997)

The chief executive of South African cricket, Ali Bacher, failed to make a planned speech in the President's Box at the Lord's Test, because he was trapped in the ladies' toilet. He had wandered in there in error to read through his notes. (1998)

Chris Purdie of Tilford dropped Gary Cox off the first ball of his over in a match against Redingensians in Surrey, and went on to concede 40 from the over. The dropped catch went for four, and Cox hit the next six balls for six. This included a no-ball, called when Purdie switched to bowling round the wicket without warning. (1998)

Two South Africans, Roger Telemachus and Geoffrey Toyana, who came to England expecting to play club cricket, were deported after arriving at Heathrow. Telemachus, who a year earlier had come to England with the

South African Test team, was allowed in for just ten days after agreeing to play for Guildford. Toyana, who had signed for Tiverton, spent ten hours in a detention cell and was then put on a plane. Both clubs insisted that the Home Office had told them a work permit was unnecessary. (1999)

"Howzat", an educational CD-Rom sent to hundreds of primary schools by the ECB, contained a hyperlink supposed to lead to a South African equipment manufacturer. In fact, it led to a pornography site operated by the Russian mafia. (2001)

Oakham Cricket Club in Rutland was hit by three arson attacks in a month. The club's pavilion was destroyed by fire over New Year, followed by the equipment store and scorebox. (2002)

An Australian batsman, Jason Taylor, playing club cricket in the West Midlands for Bewdley and also Wolverley Social, was the final victim in a hat-trick on consecutive days. (2002)

Bursledon captain Colin Popplewell wound up in hospital, nursing a gashed head, after an inadvertent assault by a team-mate during a Hampshire League match against Portsmouth Fourth Eleven. Angry after being run out, George Millward hurled his bat as he approached the boundary, knocking Popplewell out. (2002)

Rob Wade, captain of the South Wilts club in the Southern Premier League, was ruled out for the season after breaking his collarbone while competing in the fathers' sack race at a school sports day. (2003)

A cricketer in Rotorua, New Zealand, found himself fielding at deep, deep fine leg after the ground gave way beneath his feet and trapped him in a hole filled with hot water. The unnamed man, who was fielding in an inter-business match in Kuirau Park, was treated for burns. The area is full of thermal springs. (2004)

Batsman Mark Benbow missed a hundred after a hat-trick of run-outs. Benbow, playing for South Australian club West Augusta, was trying to complete his maiden A-grade century in the final over against Central-Stirling when he lost two partners off successive balls. Benbow was then last man out for 99, having instructed his partner, No. 11 Cameron Pannach, to run no matter what. (2005)

Simon Harrison, captain of Northern Counties Second Eleven in the Scottish Highlands, dropped a catch against Ross County and in the process ignited a box of matches in his pocket. He suffered minor burns; his trousers failed to recover. (2005)

Five Otago cricketers were all hit by injuries in the space of a fortnight after moving into an allegedly haunted house. Greg Todd dislocated his knee and broke his leg while bowling, Aaron Redmond dislocated his knee taking a catch, and James McMillan, Neil Broom and Jonathan Trott suffered serious muscle strains. No one else on the team was hurt. Todd said he was convinced the house, a former hospice, was to blame. "I don't think we'll be living in the same flat next year," he said. "It's all a bit spooky." Trott added that they had often found furniture and other items moved during the night. (2006)

Alok Patra had to be rescued by firemen at Poleneight, Bengal, after falling into a well while trying to retrieve a cricket ball. (2006)

In Sydney, nine Blacktown players got stuck for an hour and a quarter in a lift designed for five at teatime in their first-grade match against the University of New South Wales. They had opted to pile in rather than walk the twenty steps up to the tearoom. Rain spared the umpires from making a decision about what to do if only two fielders had walked out. (2006)

A 20-year-old man from Kandy who tried to dye his hair to look like his hero Lasith Malinga has been admitted to hospital with severe chemical burns. (2007)

The growing popularity of cricket has caused a spate of eye injuries in Mumbai. Ophthalmologist T. P. Lahane said 46% of eye injuries at the city's JJ Hospital in the past three months were caused by cricket balls, and nearly half the victims were passers-by. "In the case of ordinary accidents, there is usually scope for treatment," Lahane said, "but if a cricket ball should hit, the entire eye is damaged." (2008)

Glasgow High Kelvinside's Pakistani batsman Shahid Hameed suffered multiple fractures when immigration officials raided his flat and he jumped out of the window. Shaheed was not the target of the investigation but subsequently had his visa revoked. (2008)

Australian Julian Saye appealed for lbw so enthusiastically in a Leicestershire Senior League match that he dislocated his shoulder. Saye, playing for Birstall Village against Bharat Sports, had the consolation of getting the verdict – and returned to take two more wickets. (2009)

Lancashire wicketkeeper Gareth Cross was awarded a cut-glass trophy for the champagne moment of the season at the club awards night. He promptly dropped and smashed it. (2010) *Cross went on to play every match of Lancashire's Championship-winning season in 2011.*

The former Test batsman Dean Jones, 51, dislocated his finger when his golf club hit a tree root in his first tournament since he gained his professional card to compete on the Australian senior tour. He popped the finger back in and carried on. His caddy was Graeme Hick. (2012)

Parvez Rasool, who had made his one-day international debut for India three months earlier, found himself trapped on the top floor of his house for eleven days when floodwaters engulfed his home town of Bijbehara in Jammu & Kashmir. Rasool and his family had no phone or internet communication, and rumours spread that they were missing. He did leave the house to wade neck-deep to his car – to rescue one of his favourite bats. (2014)

County cricketer Laurie Evans had his £25,000 Mercedes stolen by a man posing as a potential purchaser. Evans was trying to sell the car prior to his move from Warwickshire to Sussex. "I started showing the car, as you do. He just drove off in it," said Evans. He was particularly upset by the loss of memorabilia signed by his former team-mates – and his best bat. (2017)

A 69-year-old man from Kalyan, near Mumbai, who believed he had won a million rupees (£12,000) in an IPL prediction competition was instead cheated out of 25,000 rupees. (2017)

... OR MAYBE NOT

A cricket injury which left a policeman in a coma for three days may have saved his life, doctors said, as they discovered he had a potentially fatal brain condition. Brain scans showed that Robert Newham, 36, from Elston, Nottinghamshire, had a malformation which would probably have killed him within fifteen years. (1998)

The family of a sick woman in Colombo said her life had been saved by the Sri Lankan TV channel showing the Mini World Cup in Dhaka. An urgent call for an A-negative blood donor was flashed on to the screen. (1998)

Dave Kachargis, 40, collapsed and died of a heart attack moments after making his highest-ever score, 139 not out. Kachargis, captain of Old Parkonians in Essex, weighed nineteen stone and was known as "Honey Monster". His wife Suzanne said: "It was the perfect way for him to go." (1999)

Carlisle Cricket Club held a minute's silence in memory of their former player and groundsman, Leonard Brunton, and then rang his home to ask if flowers should be sent. Mr Brunton answered the phone; there had been a misunderstanding. (2004)

The bad news was that 49-year-old businessman Harry Parkin collapsed on the field with a suspected heart attack almost as soon as a match in Budleigh Salterton, Devon, began. The good news was that he was guesting for a team of doctors. His team-mate Dr Richard Mejzner rushed to his car to fetch a defibrillator and may have saved his life by reviving him before the air ambulance arrived. The match was abandoned. Kevin Curran, secretary of Budleigh Salterton Cricket Club, said the club would now consider investing in a defibrillator for the pavilion. (2011)

Nine-year-old Aman Tiwari may have been saved from losing an arm because he was hurt when playing cricket. Though hit only by a tennis ball, he was in extreme pain, and doctors were able to diagnose bone cancer far earlier than would have otherwise happened. (2012)

Alan Read, 84, has regained the sight in his left eye, forty-eight years after losing it when he was struck by a cricket ball playing for East Bergholt in Suffolk. Surgeons in Yorkshire, where he now lives, reassessed the damage after Read began to get a cataract in the healthy eye and decided they could operate to reduce the pressure in the left, a procedure unknown in the 1960s. "I feel like I have a new lease of life now, and it's marvellous," he said. (2014)

MURDER AND MAYHEM

Four players from Fowey were banned by the Cornwall League after a fracas during a Division Five game at Tideford. Among them was the Fowey captain Vince Hathaway, who came on to the pitch and allegedly frogmarched umpire David Martin to the pavilion after a run-out decision. An official said it was perhaps the worst incident in the League's ninety years; the Fowey secretary, Edward Leverton, said Hathaway had only propelled the umpire backwards for about ten yards. (1993)

Police were called to a friendly village match in Northamptonshire between Brigstock and Wansford, after a Wansford batsman refused to walk when given lbw and the umpire shouted racial abuse. (1995)

A local cricketer shot dead an opponent during a match in Kashmir, after an umpire's decision went against his team. The player pulled out a revolver and fired at the opposition, killing Ghulam Hassan and wounding two others, before fleeing. (1996)

A league match in Cornwall was abandoned because of a punch-up between two players on the same side. There was a run-out with both batsmen out of their ground. Neither would leave the field, and they had to be separated by fielders after they began fighting. The batsmen, from the Barripper team, were playing a Mining Division Evening League match against Camborne. The Camborne players walked off and the game was finally abandoned when there was another incident involving the batsmen in the dressing-room. (1998)

A man was killed, and twelve injured – four seriously – in a cricket-related clash in a remote Bangladeshi village. A fight broke out in the village of Shitlai Bhabanipur as a sequel to a bad-tempered match held recently. The dead man, named as Hannan, 27, was hacked to death. A local man, Anwar Hossain, was arrested in connection with the death. (1999)

A batsman clubbed a bowler to death in a club match in Pune, India, after he appealed for lbw. Amit Shinde, 19, rushed down the pitch and hammered Atul Awachat, 23, on the head with his bat before the umpire could give his verdict. Awachat died in hospital before doctors could operate to remove a blood clot. Shinde was batting for Modern against Golden on the Fergusson College ground. (1999)

A fielder chasing a ball to the boundary in Lucknow, India, was killed by a 19-year-old youth having a driving lesson. Sanjay Misra, 22, the owner of a small bookstore, was playing with six friends in a park. (2000)

A 12-year-old boy in the Sri Lankan village of Kekanadura allegedly killed his ten-year-old brother with his bat during a dispute about the older boy's dismissal. (2000)

An Indian man was killed by an opponent during a match at Ras-al-Khaimah in the United Arab Emirates. After an argument about whether a run had been scored at a crucial stage of the match, Safi Qaffim allegedly picked up a bat and struck Labeed Mohammed on the head. He died two hours later. The two men were said to be good friends. (2000)

A village game between children in Pakistan escalated into a gunfight between their families which left five people dead. Three children, all cousins, were playing in the North-West Frontier village of Utmankhel Partas when a fight developed. One of the fathers, Shamsher Khan Bacha, reportedly saw his children being beaten up, took a gun to his uncle's house and opened fire on everyone inside. Shamsher, three of his cousins, and a mother of two died in the ensuing exchange. (2000)

A friendly in Sargodha, Pakistan, degenerated into an argument over match-fixing that culminated in two people being shot dead and five wounded. (2002)

Eleven people were arrested as police sought to quell mobs with tear gas following a riot stirred by a stray ball. Playing cricket in the road in Gomitpur near Ahmedabad, a boy hit one shot into an adjacent temple, whereupon those praying refused to return the ball, prompting the boys to throw missiles and set fire to two houses, two cars and a shop. (2003)

Three people died and thirty were injured in a riot in the Indian state of Gujarat. Communal violence broke out after Muslim boys tried to get their cricket ball back from a Hindu temple in Viramgam. (2003)

An 18-year-old youth was hit on the head with a stump and died while umpiring a game in Colombo. A 21-year-old bowler in the match was arrested. Eyewitnesses said the suspect had claimed he was bowling like Mushtaq Ahmed; the umpire, Mohamed Aboosali Pasreen, scoffed. (2004)

Two youths from the village of Santagarh, Uttar Pradesh, were murdered because the upper-caste Hasanpur cricket team resented the lower-caste Santagarh players' regular victories over them, according to civil liberties campaigners. "The cricket team from Hasanpur, made up mostly of Rajputs, seems to have taken the defeats as an insult to their pride and honour," said Pushkar Raj of the People's Union for Civil Liberties. (2004)

A group of young cricketers playing in Naroda, Ahmedabad, stumbled across twenty-three signal rockets, which are normally used by ships in distress. One was inadvertently launched, the ensuing explosion triggering panic in the streets and bringing a bomb disposal unit rushing to the field. Police were mystified as to how the rockets found their way a hundred miles inland. (2004)

Four cricketers, including a ten-year-old boy, were shot dead in the village of Doodipora, Kashmir, apparently by Indian troops trying to apprehend a suspected terrorist. The suspect escaped. (2006)

The Tamil Tigers staged an air raid on Colombo during the World Cup final, blacking out the city. Supporters who had gathered to watch Sri

Lanka play on giant screens were forced to flee in panic. No one was killed. (2007)

A man was beaten to death in India by neighbours for listening to the final between Australia and Sri Lanka. Javed Malik, 35, a jewellery designer from Thane, was listening to the radio commentary with a friend and put the set near the window for better reception. One neighbour told them to switch off the radio because India were not playing. When they refused, he broke the radio, and several others then became involved. (2007)

A match in Florida ended when a player shot an opponent with a handgun. Francis Singh underwent an emergency operation after being shot in the abdomen by opponent Devan Bascom. However, police did not arrest Bascom, saying he appeared to have been defending himself against Singh, who had threatened him with a bat. "For this man to bring a firearm to a sporting event is odd but then again, he has the right to do so," said Sergeant Spike Hopkins. "He has a concealed weapons permit and if, in fact, he was protecting himself, he was authorised by law to do so." (2007)

The pavilion at Hatch End, Middlesex, burned down hours after a mob forced the abandonment of the match between Hatch End and Old Camdenians. An anonymous player said drunken teenagers had started stealing boundary flags. This escalated until about fifty people turned up, armed with bricks and sticks, and confronted the players. Police escorted the cricketers from the ground but, according to the player, let the intruders stay. (2008)

In Cheshire, Macclesfield Cricket Club's bonfire night display raised £10,000 for club funds. After it finished, two cars were driven on to the square to perform "doughnuts" and did £3,000 worth of damage. Later that night intruders smashed up the sightscreen and threw it on the bonfire (cost: another £2,000). "It's absolutely gutting," said committee member Andrew Towle. (2010)

At least eight people were killed and fifteen injured when unidentified gunmen attacked players and spectators at an informal cricket match in the Pakistan city of Quetta. (2011)

An umpire killed a 15-year-old spectator after he ran on to the field to dispute a decision, according to police in Kishoreganj, Bangladesh. The youth, named as Nazrul Islam, rushed on after a batsman was given not out, and accused the umpire of bias. An argument ensued, then the umpire took a bat and hit the boy, who showed no immediate signs of injury but died of internal bleeding next day. The umpire, who was not named, was in hiding. (2012)

A 15-year-old was allegedly beaten to death by two of his friends after dropping a catch in a game at Lakhimpur, near Lucknow, police said. (2012)

Five Indian army privates were killed in a suicide attack on a cricket match in Bemina in disputed Kashmir. The killers entered the ground disguised as players, but had AK-47s and grenades concealed in their kit. (2013)

The Pakistani Taliban have rejected a government offer to play a cricket match for peace, saying the sport was responsible for "turning youth away from jihad". The offer came from the Interior Minister, Chaudhry Nisar Ali Khan, and provoked derision on social media. A Taliban spokesman said his group were strongly against cricket. (2014)

Ranji Trophy cricketer Harmeet Singh caused chaos by driving his car on to Platform 1 of a busy suburban railway station at Andheri, Mumbai, during the morning rush hour. No one was hurt, but Singh was charged with endangering the safety of passengers. He claimed to have taken a wrong turning. Earlier reports suggested that the player involved was the better-known Harpreet Singh, who had been hoping to attract bids in the IPL auction, which was starting the same morning. By the time a correction was issued, it was too late. (2017) *Harpreet later got a chance as a replacement for Royal Challengers Bangalore.*

A 12-year-old boy in Howrah, West Bengal, was apparently killed by a friend after a dispute over a 250-rupee (£3) cricket bet, police said. The victim apparently won the bet but the other boy, also 12, refused to pay, triggering a quarrel which ended with him smashing the other's head with a brick before hiding the body in nearby jungle. (2017)

A farmer died in Amroli, Gujarat, after being struck by a bat for refusing to return a ball that had been hit on to his land, police said. They were hunting for a missing 20-year-old man. (2017)

Delhi police said a teenage cricketer killed passer-by Angad Gupta, 22, with his bat after Gupta had protested about being struck by a ball hit out of a nearby park. (2017)

A 15-year-old umpire was taken to hospital after allegedly being head-butted by a spectator while officiating in an Under-11 match in the Melbourne suburb of Sunshine North. A witness said he was attacked after telling a group of spectators to stop drinking alcohol during a match between Sunshine and Caroline Springs. (2017)

NEIGHBOURS

Batsmen at the Melbourne Town club, Derbyshire, have been asked not to hit sixes on one side of the pitch to avoid irritating residents in a new housing development. Cricket has been played on the ground since 1920; the houses were erected in 1996. (1997)

Two clubs have been told they must bat at only one end of the ground at Littleover, Derbyshire. Littleover Centurions and St Augustine's were said to be hitting too many balls out of the ground into nearby properties. (2000)

Lambeth Council banned a performance by reggae star Beanie Man at one of the lunch intervals during the Oval Test – for fear of annoying residents. "It's incredibly petty," said a spokesman for Channel 4, under whose aegis Beanie Man was going to appear. (2000)

Mark Portsmouth, chairman of Mumbles Cricket Club in Swansea, offered £100 to the first player to hit a ball into the garden of the house being bought by the privacy-obsessed actors Michael Douglas and Catherine Zeta-Jones, 150 yards away. To win, the successful smiter had to ask for the ball back. (2003)

Shamley Green Cricket Club, in Surrey, have been forced to cease awarding sixes for balls hit on to the property of neighbour Mike Burgess after threats of legal action. Mr Burgess, who moved in to the house in 2005, claimed twenty-four tiles had been broken and his elderly mother-in-law nearly hit. Shamley Green have played on the village green since 1840. "If you don't like klaxons and sirens," said club president Tony Hodgson, "you don't move next to a fire station." (2006)

East Northamptonshire County Council forced Rushden Town Cricket Club to commission a £2,000 survey to prove that the addition of new nets would not annoy residents, even though none of the people in the nearest fifty houses had complained. Club secretary Chris Layram said the only complaints came after an Abba tribute night, organised to raise funds to pay for the survey. (2008)

Craig Smith, who lives in a flat near the Middlesbrough Cricket Club ground at Acklam Park, decided to play a joke on his girlfriend by pretending that a rogue cricket ball had just hit a friend on the head. Smith said: "Within ten minutes of me winding her up, there was a crash and bang in the flat. I looked around and there was another cricket ball spinning on the kitchen floor. It's weird, like the boy who cried wolf or something." Lol Davison, chairman of the cricket club, said such incidents were very rare: a forty-foot net was erected when the flats were built. (2008)

The last cricket pitch in the London Borough of Islington (population: 195,000) has been saved, after being threatened with closure when a Porsche driver successfully sued the council for the cost of a broken window. Councillors agreed to erect extra netting at Wray Crescent, home of Pacific Cricket Club. Club secretary Peter Hollman said: "The residents are really happy to have us because we keep the gangs away, but there's one guy who hates us. He's got a Porsche and two other flash cars, and any time the ball goes near them he takes it and refuses to give it back." (2011)

Charlie Elphicke, the Conservative MP for Dover, told people living next to the village cricket ground at St Margaret's to stop complaining about broken windows and buy stronger glass. Residents had demanded that the club erect a thirty-foot fence. "The cricket club has been there for a very long time," said Elphicke. "Those houses have not. They bought these houses knowing there was a cricket club." (2013)

An insurance company sent a $NZ759 bill to a 15-year-old boy, Taine Forster, after he hit a ball out of a Wellington park and dented a car. His mother Carole said if kids or their parents were held liable in such cases,

"they'll just stop playing sport". The claim was dropped after a newspaper rang the insurers. (2014)

Britwell Salome Cricket Club in Oxfordshire were forced to ban sixes at one end and spend £4,000 on a 50-foot net after complaints by neighbour Diana Attenborough, 69. They then discovered she had put her house up for sale. "We have been in the village for over eighty-five years," said chairman Nigel Joyner. "In all that time we have not had any complaints other than those from Diana." (2014)

Residents of a new estate bordering the ground at Feethams, where Darlington Cricket Club have played since 1866, objected to a new all-weather practice area, citing the noise created in net sessions. They complained about the sound of bat on ball and also about bowlers grunting. One letter took issue with men "dropping their trousers to remove thigh-pads and boxes in their underwear". Councillors later agreed training could continue as long as the club reduced their hours and the sessions were "properly supervised". (2017)

A Mumbai family have sought refuge in Dubai after falling out with their neighbours because their son damaged a car's windscreen wiper while playing cricket in the car park of an upmarket residential complex. "We couldn't face the harassment and torture anymore," said Anil D'Souza, father of 13-year-old Aryan. "We cannot stay in a place where people are jealous and violent and do not like children."(2017)

NOSTALGIA

Lob bowling was compulsory for one bowler on either side in a match at West Wycombe between The Sherlock Holmes Society of London, and The P. G. Wodehouse Society (UK). The Sherlockians' challenge called for 1895 Laws to apply – on the grounds that Sherlock Holmes once declared: "It is always 1895." Five-ball overs and eight-inch wickets were duly restored. (2001)

Etchingham & Fontridge Cricket Club, Sussex, has been re-formed after a 67-year hiatus. The first ball for the new club was bowled by Matt Neve, whose grandfather had bowled the final delivery in 1939, before war led to the club's disappearance. (2006)

Kirriemuir, the town north of Dundee where J. M. Barrie was born, helped celebrate the 150th anniversary of its most famous son by re-enacting a match played when Barrie opened the sports pavilion in 1930. Among those present to watch Kirriemuir play the Wayward Gentlemen was Leslie Kettles, 85, who watched his father open the batting in the original 1930 match. "I could hardly see Barrie for dignitaries," he recalled. (2010)

The P. G. Wodehouse Society held a brunch during the Cheltenham Cricket Festival to mark the centenary of Gloucestershire's match against Warwickshire, attended by the young Wodehouse, at which he was rather taken with the surname of one Warwickshire player: P. Jeeves. (2013)

Tom Smith, the opening bowler for Birchencliffe Cricket Club, re-enacted a historic cricketing feat by throwing a cricket ball over the Lockwood railway viaduct near Huddersfield. The viaduct is 129 feet high and 30 feet wide, but Smith estimated a height of 180 feet was necessary to get sufficient carry. It is also important to consult the train timetable. Watched by a *Huddersfield Daily Examiner* reporter and photographer, he succeeded at the first attempt. (2013)

Bill Boon, 78, was given a round of applause at Netley School, the London Borough of Camden's oldest primary – seventy years late. As an eight-year-old, Boon took six wickets in a school match and was excited at the prospect of having his name read out in assembly next day. But he was hit on the shins when batting and had to take a day off sick. He had returned to the school on its 130th anniversary, and the current generation made good the omission. (2013)

Auctioneers and solicitors in Colchester played a nostalgic match against each other to mark the centenary of a fixture contested days before the outbreak of the First World War. The solicitors, soundly beaten in 1914, won the rematch, which raised £5,500 for local charities. (2014)

A game in Buckinghamshire left uncompleted when war was declared in 1914 was finally replayed a century later. The fixture between The Lee Cricket Club, near Great Missenden, and the village's Manor House was abandoned because of rain on August 3, 1914, the day before Britain declared war on Germany. The players said they would finish it off after the fighting. They never did: three of the village team – Albert Phillips and brothers Arthur and Ralph Brown – were killed, and several others wounded. The game was staged as a tribute to the fallen, with ceremonies led by Elizabeth Stewart-Liberty, whose father-in-law Ivor had been captain of the original Manor House team. (2014)

Patrick Dewing and Steven Matthews broke the 27-year-old opening partnership record for Bradenham Cricket Club, in Norfolk, with 228 against Swardeston B. The previous record, 180, was set by the same two batsmen in 1989. (2016)

Battle Cricket Club in Sussex marked the 950th anniversary of the Norman Conquest by welcoming a team of French Barbarians, restricted to French-born players, to compete for the Guillaume Trophy. The French lost, but creditably. (2016)

POLITICS

The former Government minister John Redwood, who challenged John Major for the Conservative Party leadership in 1995, led a team of "Eurosceptics" to a five-wicket win over a team of "Europhiles", captained by Lord Archer, at Burton's Court, London. (1996)

Former Labour leader Neil Kinnock, now a European Commissioner, resigned as honorary president of the Royal Brussels Cricket Club after members complained that he had failed to attend a match or social function in his two years in office. (1997)

The Conservative Party, struggling in the opinion polls, has identified cricket followers – along with those who enjoy rugby, tennis, art and gardening – as potential supporters. They have bought membership lists from cricket clubs with a view to a direct-mail recruitment drive. (1999)

Constitutional expert Professor Peter Hennessy said he was told by a civil servant that the greatest threat to Britain's national security occurred at the height of the Cold War, during the thrilling finish to the 1963 Lord's Test: "Every television screen in the Ballistic Early Warning System room was tuned to Lord's. The Russians could have taken us out at any time." (2000)

Ian Botham agreed to head a team of sporting figures in an advertising campaign against replacing the pound with the euro. "I played for England," said Botham, "not Europe." (2002)

Paul Kelleher failed in his attempt to use a cricket bat to disfigure a £150,000 statue of former prime minister Margaret Thatcher, so he reached instead for a metal stanchion, and decapitated it. The bat just "pinged off" her head, he said. Kelleher, who was found guilty of criminal damage, said the offence was "an act of satirical humour" directed at global capitalism. He was later jailed for three months. (2002)

Cricketers have complained that one of Mumbai's historic grounds, Shivaji Park, is being destroyed by constant political rallies. "The pitch is a minefield, the outfield is dangerous and the schedule is in a mess," said coach Amar Vaidya. (2007)

Martin McGuinness, former senior member of the Provisional IRA and now deputy first minister of Northern Ireland, has confessed to a lifelong enthusiasm for cricket. "There are many closet cricket fans in the nationalist community," he said. (2007) *See also 2015.*

The annual grudge match between opposing parties on Ealing Council was cancelled when the Conservatives refused to play in protest against Labour attacks on the Tory mayor. "It's a way of saying their behaviour is not acceptable," said Conservative leader Jason Stacey. The Labour MP for Ealing North, Steve Pound, said: "I don't believe in mixing sport and politics. I suppose the fact we beat them last time doesn't have any bearing on it." (2009)

BBC broadcaster John Simpson has unearthed claims that Hitler wanted to use cricket to prepare German soldiers for war. In his new book, *Unreliable Sources*, Simpson cites a 1930 article in the *Daily Mirror* claiming that Hitler was taught the game by British PoWs during the First World War but declared it "insufficiently violent" for his purposes. In particular, he wanted to abolish pads, which he considered "unmanly and unGerman". (2010)

Britain's new prime minister David Cameron talked enthusiastically about his love of cricket at a reception for the England squad who won the World Twenty20 in Barbados. However, his credibility was somewhat dented when he called captain Paul Collingwood "Colin" and gave the impression that he thought the final had been at Kennington Oval rather than Kensington Oval. (2010)

The former England fast bowler Darren Gough, 40, turned down a personal request from the prime minister, David Cameron, to stand as the Conservative candidate in the Barnsley Central by-election. Gough thought it was a hoax call and hung up. He later agreed to campaign for the party, but said he was too busy to contemplate being an MP. (2011)

Officials at Trent Bridge strategically wheeled a sightscreen into position to protect Nick Clegg, the unpopular deputy prime minister, from protesters when he arrived for a meeting with colleagues. (2012)

The pavilion at Malpas Cricket Club, on the outskirts of Newport, South Wales, achieved an unbeatable niche in political history when it was used as a polling station in Britain's first elections for police commissioners, and no voters at all turned up. Council officials waited in vain for fourteen hours for any of the 8,278 electors in Bettws Ward to exercise their democratic rights. Turnout nationally was about 15%, a record low. (2012)

Sixty-seven students from the disputed Indian state of Jammu & Kashmir were suspended and threatened with charges of sedition for supporting the wrong team in the India–Pakistan Asia Cup match. The incident happened at a university in Meerat, Uttar Pradesh. Omar Abdullah, chief minister of Jammu & Kashmir, intervened on their behalf, saying the charges were "unacceptably harsh", although the students "needed to introspect". (2014)

Home Secretary Theresa May, a candidate to be a future Conservative leader, has named Geoff Boycott as one of her heroes. "I have been a Boycott fan all my life," she said. "He kind of solidly got on with what he was doing." (2014)

Government officials have blocked an attempt by Home Secretary Theresa May to award Geoff Boycott a knighthood. The Cabinet Office cited Boycott's 1996 conviction in France for assaulting his then lover. The campaign was led by Conservative backbench MPs, but Mrs May lent her name to it. She couldn't get past the civil servants, though. One of the MPs, Nigel Adams, said: "It sounds as if some jobsworth numpty who doesn't understand Geoffrey's contribution to sport has let his pen get carried away." (2015)

Martin McGuinness, the Republican leader who is now Northern Ireland's Deputy First Minister, dressed up as W. G. Grace in a fundraising stunt for a children's hospice. McGuinness, an ardent cricket fan, said: "I always admired the ability of a man to stand at a crease and take on all comers." (2015)

Natalie Bennett, the former journalist who leads the British Green Party, received an email two days before the general election asking about her availability for *The Times* cricket team's fixture the following Saturday. Bennett kept wicket for the team when she worked for the paper. Despite the timing, she replied within twenty minutes, giving apologies "due to the possibility of being in a non-smoke-filled room", thrashing out a coalition deal. (2015) *In the event the Conservatives won an overall majority, and the Greens just one seat, so she could have played.*

Cricket teams in the Kashmir Valley are causing political concerns because they are being named after militants opposed to India's control of the disputed region. "If this practice is not nipped in the bud, it can create a huge problem in coming months and years," said a security official. "The psyche of the impressionable minds is sought to be influenced." (2016)

A councillor in Westbury, Tasmania (pop: 1,500), has suggested changing the name of the local cricket ground to the Donald J. Trump Park. "It is in our best interests to extend the hand of friendship to the new president of the United States, who is not a politician and will likely come at things from a different perspective," said Councillor John Temple. The response, Temple said later, had been mixed. "The personal conversations I have had have all been positive," he said. "I have seen things on Facebook calling me an idiot." (2016)

PRODIGIES

Andrew Flintoff, 15, a pupil at Ribbleton Hall High School, Preston, hit 234 not out in only 20 overs with 20 sixes and 20 fours, for St Anne's against Fulwood & Broughton. (1993)

Simon Penny, ten, took eight wickets in 11 overs for Stogumber, Somerset, against Roadwater. He normally plays for the club Under-13s but was called into the first team at the last minute. He missed the after-match celebrations because it was past his bedtime. (1993)

Paul Johnston made his debut for Blackhall Thirds against Preston in the North Yorkshire & South Durham League, aged six. The team were a man short and in danger of being fined before Paul was drafted in by his father. Wearing his own pad, gloves and helmet, he batted almost six overs in a last-wicket stand and scored a single. (1995)

David Winn, aged ten, saved Mirfield Parish Cavaliers from relegation in the Central Yorkshire League after being called in when the side were short. He shared a last-wicket stand of 28 to give his team victory over Thornhill. (1995)

Deepak Choughale, a 12-year-old schoolboy, scored 400 not out in Karnataka's 589 for four against Goa in a two-day match in the Sportstar Under-13 tournament in Madras. He batted 316 minutes, and was given a bicycle as a reward. (1996)

William Bruce, aged nine, took ten wickets in an innings with his leg-breaks for King's Junior School, Canterbury, for the second year running. This time he had figures of ten for 36 – including five stumpings – in an Under-11s match against Wellesley House School. (1997)

Ten-year-old Michael Andrews scored 241 not out in 100 minutes for Birchfield Prep School, Shropshire, against Belmont School from Surrey. He hit 11 sixes and 30 fours, and was rewarded by being let off his homework. His mother said that both Michael and his 12-year-old brother John Philip are cricket-crazy: "They eat, sleep and drink cricket. Whenever there's an English batting collapse, friends say to the boys: 'Hurry up and get in the team.'" (1998)

Thirteen-year-old American Nicholas de la Motte took eight wickets for nought for Hurstpierpoint College, bowling medium-pace, less than three months after joining the school and playing his first match. Stoke Brunswick were bowled out for 15. Nicholas said he wanted to take up cricket as a career and play for Sussex and England. (1998)

Nine-year-old George Ledden, playing his third game of cricket, took four wickets in four balls for Rottingdean in an East Sussex League Under-12 game against Newhaven. (1999)

Mignon du Preez, a 12-year-old schoolgirl from Pretoria, scored 258 not out, including 16 sixes, in a 40-over provincial Under-13 game for Gauteng North against Gauteng at Sandton. Her father, Jacques, said she fell in love with the game as a four-year-old. (2002) *She made her debut for South Africa's national team in 2007, and later captained them.*

In Yorkshire, ten-year-old leg-spinner Bradley Williamson took six wickets in seven balls, including two hat-tricks, playing for Spen Victoria Under-11s against Lightcliffe. (2006)

Ten-year-old off-spinner Jacob Smith took a hat-trick playing among the grown-ups in Seaford Fourth Eleven's first-ever Sussex League fixture. He finished the match with four Hellingly wickets for eight. "I wish I'd brought him on earlier," said captain Simon Pitts. (2007)

Ten-year-old Sarfaraz Khan scored 200 not out for Payyade Sports Club against the D. Y. Patil Cricket Academy in an Under-13 match in Mumbai. (2007) *He later played first-class cricket, and in the IPL.*

A 13-year-old boy scored 401 at the Mumbai Cricket Association's Under-14 summer camp. Ramanpreet Singh Ghuman led Navi Mumbai from 130 for seven to 555 for nine against Bhayandar. Interviewed afterwards by the press, he displayed a broad range of interests. What is your ambition? "To be a cricketer." Do you watch anything on television? "Yes, cricket." Any other sport you like? "Only cricket, nothing else." Hobbies? "Playing cricket."(2008)

Kyle Pittman took all ten wickets in 17 balls in an Under-13 match for City of London School against Haberdashers' Knights Academy. He finished with figures of 2.5–1–1–10. "I just bowled them full and straight," he said. (2008)

George Pearson, 11, took six wickets in an over playing only his fourth game of cricket, for Milnthorpe Under-13s against Bolton-le-Sands. Coach Chris Baldwin, who had been teaching George to bowl spin, said he could not believe his eyes. (2008)

Dominic Sibley, 13-year-old son of former ECB commercial director Mark Sibley, hit six sixes off the last over of Whitgift School Under-13s' innings against Harris School. (2009) *In 2013, aged 18 and playing for Surrey, he was the youngest to score a double-century in the County Championship. He later joined Warwickshire.*

Twelve-year-old Mark Vincent took seven wickets in seven balls – in his first competitive game of cricket. Playing for Grosvenor Grammar School in Northern Ireland against Parkhall, he took the wickets in his first two overs. His father Ivan said Mark had no idea that he had done anything remarkable: "He was a bit downbeat when we asked him how he got on, telling us he had only scored two. It was only when his brother Drew asked about the bowling that the story of the seven wickets came out." (2009)

Ten-year-old South African leg-spinner David Blenkinsop has taken a hat-trick of hat-tricks, achieving the feat in three consecutive matches. Playing for Middelburg Primary's Under-11s he stormed through the three matches with combined figures of ten for five in five overs. David, whose hero is Shane Warne, practises for an hour and a half every day. (2009)

In Queensland, Holly Ferling, 13, an emergency selection for the Kingaroy Services senior men's team playing South Burnett Warriors, took a hat-trick with her first three balls, and a fourth wicket with her fifth ball. Warriors captain Paul Clegg described her bowling as "brilliant". (2010) *In 2013, still only 17, she was part of the Australian squad that won the women's World Cup.*

Seven-year-old Charlie Allison from Colchester has become an internet sensation after the release on YouTube of a video of him batting in the nets, driving, pulling and reverse-sweeping with near-professional aplomb. (2012)

Eleven-year-old Kieran Gray of Maidenhead & Bray's Under-13s took the first six Taplow wickets in an over – and was then taken off to allow his team-mates to bowl. His figures thus remained 1–1–0–6. His first five victims were bowled, the last caught at cover. Taplow, 21 all out, lost by 131 runs. (2012)

Nine-year-old Josh Griffiths from Northop, Flintshire, took five wickets in five balls, while having treatment for leukaemia. Playing for Northop Under-9s against Denbigh, he took five for one from two overs. Three days earlier, he had endured his latest bout of chemotherapy. He tries to play cricket three times a week and, during his intensive treatment in 2012 when cricket was impossible, the club messaged him continually to keep him in touch. His coach Roy Pierce said: "He loves to stay in the game all the time." (2013)

Six-year-old Harrison Parsons outscored his father when he opened the batting for Abercarn Cricket Club, in Monmouthshire, against a side put out by the village football team. Dad Jeremy made 15, Harrison 24. "It's a bit of a rivalry between the teams, and was a highly contested match. Obviously, I'm pleased as punch for him," said Jeremy. His mum, Beki, said: "Since he was two, all Harrison has done is play cricket. When I had cartoons on for him on the telly, he

would get the remote and change it to the sports channels to see the cricket." (2013)

An eight-year-old York girl, Mollie Ovenden, was named Junior Voice of Cricket after winning a competition organised by Yorkshire for Under-15s. Entrants had to submit their own commentary to a clip of Yorkshire cricket. In the final, Mollie interviewed the bowler Jack Brooks, and asked him: "What two things did Alastair Cook retain at Old Trafford?" Then she gleefully revealed: "The answer was the Ashes and my pen, because he kept it after signing my autograph book."(2013)

Thomas Wrigglesworth, aged ten, took five for nine with his "looping leggies" in a Victorian senior fourth-grade match for Sale against Stratford. It was his second senior appearance, but the first time he had attempted leg-spin in a match. "He was a wicketkeeper last year," said his father Ian, who played for Victoria in the 1990s. "And he's just decided the leggies were worth a try, and pestered everyone enough to the point where he was given a bowl." He refused to be drawn about the chances of his son following him into first-class cricket: "We were more inclined to talk about the duck he made in the morning. We're not going to pump him up."(2015)

Eight-year-old Luke Marsh from Dunedin dismissed six batsmen in an over, every one of them bowled, for Kaikorai. He never got the chance for more because the opposition, Taieri, were all out for one in two overs. "It didn't seem real when the ball kept hitting the wickets," Luke's mum Michelle said. It was his first year of hard-ball cricket, having started playing when he was five. Asked by the BBC if he had always been good, Luke replied: "Hmmmm… yeah." (2016)

... OR MAYBE NOT

Bone-density tests initiated by India's cricket board, which are supposed to be able to measure young people's age accurately, have shown that many Under-16 players are over-age. Of thirty-two probables for Mumbai's Under-16 team, eleven were said to be ineligible; similar numbers were reported elsewhere. (2012)

... AND TOO MANY OF THEM

India's National Commission on Population used the one-day internationals against England to launch a birth control campaign, complete with the slogans "Little bouncers – no more please", "No slips please, population control is not a laughing matter", and "China stumped – India produced more babies in the last hour!"(2002)

PROTESTS

There were 75 wides in Aruna's winning total of 158 for one in a Sri Lankan second division match against Old Servatius. The wides were bowled deliberately in protest against an appeal for a catch being disallowed. (2002)

Khaled Mahmud, the Bangladesh Test player, showed his displeasure at being dismissed in a one-day Ispahani National League encounter by slapping the bowler. (2002)

Cricket fans held a rally against a ruling by the Maharashtra government ending an old rule preventing clubs holding more than thirty weddings a year. There is now no limit, providing the clubs pay the state 25,000 rupees (£320) each time. Cricketers objected that endless weddings would eat into the seven months that grounds are available for the game after the monsoon. "We have around eighty registered tournaments," said Mumbai Cricket Association secretary Lalchand Rajput. "How will we manage to conduct these?" (2005)

Bryan Pietersen, brother of the more famous Kevin, "went bananas", according to opponents, after having an lbw appeal turned down in a Southampton evening match between Trant and Otters. After Trant had scored 186 from their 16 overs, Pietersen took two wickets with his first two balls before embarking on a campaign of remonstrating with the umpire. "I could have understood it," said one Otters player, "but we were 17 for four at the time." (2005)

Gloucester-based side Walls Crescent jumped into their cars and went home after an lbw decision, given by the local vicar, went against them in a Gloucestershire League match at Westbury. "We just thought it would be better for us to pack up and go home before things got much worse," said the Walls Crescent secretary M. Fadra. The club did, however, offer to pay for their uneaten teas. (2006)

Groundstaff at Eden Gardens in Calcutta have threatened suicide unless they get a pay rise. (2008)

Hindu nationalists rampaged through Mumbai, tearing up film posters and stoning a cinema, after Bollywood star Shahrukh Khan expressed regret that no Pakistanis were playing in the Indian Premier League. (2010)

Congress Party supporters in Rajkot dug up the pitch at the Madhavrao Scindia Cricket Ground, which has hosted twelve one-day internationals, to protest against the use of water during a drought. The stadium was being prepared for an inter-municipal corporation Twenty20 tournament. "The city is facing a drinking-water crisis," said the protesters' leader Atul Rajani. "If they want to organise it, they should have organised it in some other city." (2013)

Lalmatia bowler Sujon Mahmud conceded 92 runs in the opening over of an innings in the Dhaka League Second Division. He gave away 65 wides (from 13 wide balls) and 15 from three no-balls before opponents Axiom passed the 89 they needed for a ten-wicket win. Lalmatia were protesting against decisions taken by the umpires when they were all out for 88. Lalmatia general secretary Adnan Rahman Dipon said the problems began at the toss: "My captain was not allowed to see the coin. We were sent to bat first and as expected, the umpires' decisions came against us." In a similar incident Tasnim Hasan of Fear Fighters conceded 69 off seven balls. The Bangladesh Cricket Board were unimpressed by the grievances: they banned both bowlers for ten years for "tarnishing the image of Bangladesh cricket"; several club officials were banned for five, and the teams were suspended from the league indefinitely. (2017)

REIGN OF TERROR

A Muslim terrorist group, the Al-Umar Mujahideen, said it tried to kidnap the former Indian captain, Kapil Dev, in 1996 to try to secure the release of the group's leader from an Indian jail. "Our plans didn't work out," said a spokesman. (2000)

Relatives of Omar Khyam, the captain of the Sussex Under-18 team, went to Pakistan to search for him in terrorist training camps. Khyam, from Crawley, had been studying for his A-levels when he was recruited by a militant Islamic group. (2000) *In 2007 Khyam was jailed for life for conspiring to cause explosions in Britain. He was described as "ruthless, devious, artful and dangerous" by the judge at the Old Bailey, who warned that he might never be released.*

Cricket balls were banned on Indian internal flights as part of the post-September 11 security clampdown. British Airways has banned bats on flights to the United States. (2001)

The bomb squad was called to a *Wisden* reader's house in the US after the posted copy of his 2001 Almanack was identified as a suspicious package. (2002)

Cricket bats – along with axes, baseball bats, box-cutters, brass knuckles, bull whips, cattle prods, corkscrews, golf clubs and numchucks [ninja weapons] – were on a new list of implements banned from American aircraft cabins (2002)

Pinky and Vasu Desai were left unmoved by the attack on the Akshardham temple complex near Ahmedabad, which killed at least 30 people. Although the couple were inside the temple at the time, they assumed the noise was merely a series of firecrackers going off in celebration of a victory by the Indian cricket team. (2002)

Muslim militants arrested in Jammu, northern India, were found to have concealed cash, a wireless handset and 120 bullets inside cricket bats. (2003)

The Great Preston team has been fined £100 by the Wetherby League after Asian opponents were allegedly jeered as "Al-Qaeda members" by supporters. The league chairman, Zahid Ali, resigned in protest at the leniency of the fine. (2003)

The former Australian Test batsman Dean Jones was sacked as a commentator by Ten Sports after he called South African batsman Hashim Amla "a terrorist". Thinking he was off-mike, Jones said "The terrorist has got another wicket" when Amla, a bearded Muslim, took a catch in a one-day international against Sri Lanka in Colombo. "I'm gone. I'm on the 1am flight," Jones told journalists. "It was a silly and completely insensitive thing to say and, obviously, it was never supposed to be heard over the air." (2006)

The London bombers who perpetrated the terrorist attacks of July 7, 2005, were originally ordered by Al-Qaeda to murder the England and Australia cricket teams, a friend of one of the bombers claimed. They were told to get jobs as stewards at Edgbaston during the Second Test and spray sarin gas in the dressing-rooms, he said. The friend added that one of the plotters, Shahzad Tanweer, objected to the plan because he was a cricketer. (2006)

A Sri Lankan government official announced the news of the death of the rebel Tamil Tiger leader Prahbhakaran with the following words: "Match Over, series won, captain's wicket gone, stumps drawn, players heading for pavilion. That's all I can say for now." (2009)

King's Circle in Mumbai was closed for an hour as bomb disposal units and dogs examined a cricket ball embedded with the dial of a watch which had been left by a tree. It turned out to be an IPL souvenir. (2012)

Hajji Khubi, father of Afghanistan captain Mohammad Nabi, was kidnapped outside his home in Jalalabad and held captive for more than two months. He was released and no ransom paid, the provincial governor's office said. Two people were arrested, but no group claimed responsibility. (2013)

The unit of the New York Police Department set up to spy on potential terrorists after the 9/11 outrage in 2001 compiled a list of hot-spots in the city where Muslim men gathered, including cricket grounds. In a new book, *Enemies Within*, reporters Matt Apuzzo and Adam Goldman revealed that police were also advised to keep an eye on "cricket fan hangouts", such as Singh's Sporting Goods on 101st Avenue and the New Neimat Kada Restaurant on Lexington Avenue. (2013)

The New York Police Department has abolished a unit that spied on cricket grounds and other venues frequented by Muslims in an attempt to gather intelligence about possible terrorist attacks. The force admitted the programme, set up after 9/11, had not generated a single lead. (2014)

RELATIVITY

Father and son Mahindra and Ajoy Gokal both scored unbeaten centuries in the same innings for Luton Exiles against Langford Second Eleven. (1995)

Nick Causton, 14, took two hat-tricks in an innings for Brooke Under-18s against Loddon in Norfolk, emulating a feat achieved by his late grandfather, Sidney Causton, for another Norfolk team, Mundford, in 1922. Nick kept the ball his grandfather had used on a shelf in his bedroom. (1996)

Alan Drew, 65, and his 14-year-old grandson, James Docherty, shared a century opening stand for Penarth in a Third Eleven fixture against Pontypridd. (1996)

A reunion of members of a family called Alston, at Bere Alston, Devon, included a game between 11 Alstons and the village team. (1996)

A team of Blanks played a match against Staffordshire club Cannock Wood, when Alan Blank, a member of the club, put together an eleven entirely composed of his relatives. It filled in a blank day in the club fixture list. There were eight Blanks and three relations with a different surname. Two of the team, father and son, were both called David Blank. Another Blank umpired, and other clan members provided what the club said was a record attendance. (1998)

Father and daughter Jim and Tracey Dixon umpired the Westmorland League match between Sedgwick and Burnside. (1999)

Chris Hayman caught his brother Courtney off their father Carlton's bowling in a match between Indian Wanderers and Highway Third

Eleven in Coventry. The scorebook thus read: C. Hayman c C. Hayman b C. Hayman 3. (1999)

Eighteen-year-old Martin Hall scored a century with his mother as his batting partner. Martin was on 96, playing for Bredon against Ashton under Hill in Worcestershire, when the seventh wicket fell and his mother Alison came in. Alison, 41, normally works behind the club bar but had agreed to make up the numbers because the team were three men short. The partnership remained unbroken: she made two, he made 108. (1999)

Brothers Tom, 22, and Ben Tebbutt, 26, both claimed hat-tricks for West Bridgfordians in a South Notts League match against Farndon. Ben completed his feat when, as captain, he brought himself on for a single over. All six victims were bowled. Cricket historian Peter Wynne-Thomas could recall only one parallel, by the Barnard brothers in a 1954 house match at Cranleigh School, Surrey. (2001)

All twenty-two players, and one scorer, in a match in Bradford between Yorkshire LPS and Amarmilan were named Patel. "Some of us are related," said Chandu Patel, the Amarmilan secretary and medium-pacer. "We used to have a player called Mahmood, but he got married and only plays when we're very short." (2001)

Brothers John and Andy Lyne got the same score on the same day in different matches, and were out exactly the same way. They were opening the batting in games ten miles apart, and each hit 101 before being bowled leg stump. Both were playing for Yorkshire village Anston against Whitwell, John captaining the First Eleven and Andy the seconds. (2002)

Mohammed Kaif's parents and brother, back home in Allahabad, were so convinced India were about to lose a one-day international against England at Lord's that they went to the cinema to see the Bollywood tear-jerker *Devdas* and missed his match-winning 87 not out. "Someone told us midway through the film that India had won and that Kaif had played a great innings," said his brother Saif, also a first-class cricketer. (2002)

Three generations of Barretts played in a tour match at Barrow for the Aberdeenshire club Ellon Gordon: Hayden Barrett, his son Jon and grandson Sam. (2003)

In Herefordshire, identical twins Steve and Stuart Evans, 33, captained the opposing teams in a Marches League match between Ledbury and Bartestree & Lugwardine. Steve is a right-handed batsman who bowls left-arm; Stuart is a left-handed batsman who bowls right-arm. (2003)

Jason Phillips dismissed three members of the Dredge clan when he took a hat-trick for Knowle against Frome in a Somerset Cup tie. He dismissed the former Somerset county player, Colin Dredge – "the Demon of Frome" – then Colin's brother, Craig, and his nephew, Neil. (2000)

The captains in the Bolton Association local derby between Atherton and Astley & Tyldesley were father and son, Steve and Paul Walsh. (2005)

Quentin Jones and his ten-year-old son Martin led Olney Town Second Eleven to a remarkable win over Milton Bryan. Olney, needing 94 to win, had collapsed to 76 for nine when Martin joined his father. The pair

batted together for 12.3 overs before Quentin hit the winning four; Martin scored five not out despite having all the fielders round the bat. (2007)

The Cornish family Strick had an extraordinary afternoon in the Cornwall League. Martin Strick took a hat-trick and scored 41 for Redruth against Bude in the first division, before hearing that his brother Adrian had hit a career-best 87 for the second team. Meanwhile, in Division Six, their father Tony scored 60 not out for Stithians Second Eleven, helped by his 15-year-old nephew Nathan – who joined him at the crease to clinch victory with an unbeaten 32 – plus Nathan's father Roger who had earlier taken five for 24. Tony's wife Mandy said: "One of the parents watching the game at Stithians asked if I could bottle the genes." (2007)

Three fathers and daughters played together in Whitland's third team against Hook Second Eleven in Division Five of the Pembrokeshire League: Colin and Alice John, Gwyn and Rachel Phillips, and Ashley and Nerys Evans. Whitland lost after Hook's Samantha Rossiter took four for 12. (2008)

Twin brothers Nazim and Zahid Mohammad have been banned after successfully pulling off an identity switch during an inter-league match. Nazim was picked as a bowler for the Liverpool & District Competition against the Nottinghamshire Premier League but brother Zahid, the better batsman, took his place at the crease when Nazim's turn came. Officials failed to notice at the time – since Zahid made nought, there was not much time to notice – but word leaked out later. The brothers have now left their club, New Brighton. (2009)

The Dewsbury Young Stars turned out an all-Patel team against Warwick, who also included three Patels – leading to a dismissal reading Patel c Patel b Patel 27. "It's just a coincidence," insisted club secretary Yunus Patel. (2009)

All fifteen players (plus the manager) in the Twirupa Brai High School Under-16 squad at the Polly Umrigar national schools competition had the same surname: Jamatia. They all belong to the same tribe in Tripura.

The Tripura state senior women's team also fielded a team of Jamatias in a tournament. (2010)

Saqlain Mushtaq, the Pakistan off-spinner who played in the 1999 World Cup, locked his wife in a cupboard the night before the final to avoid disciplinary action. She had to hide after team officials, who had banned families from the latter stages of the tournament, knocked on the door of his London hotel room. Then the coach and other players turned up and, said Saqlain, "unfortunately her wait to come out became a long one". Pakistan lost to Australia next day by nine wickets. (2011)

A father and son took five wickets each in an innings for Goonellabah Workers Sports against Southern Cross University at Bexhill, New South Wales. Michael Mansfield, 56, took the first five wickets for five. He was replaced after his maximum five overs by his 17-year-old son Kody, who claimed the remaining wickets for 16. The university were 51 all out and lost by 29 runs. (2012)

Bowling seam-up, Jackson Warne, 14, took four wickets in five balls, including a hat-trick, for the Year Ten team at Brighton Grammar School. His better-known father, Shane, was watching: "Jackson did it!!!!" he tweeted. Jackson had previously preferred football to cricket. (2015)

The Redruth fourth team, playing Grampound Road in the Cornish League Division Six West, included club president Mark Richards, 47, plus his son, wife and two daughters. There was no case of c Richards b Richards but, said Mark, "We did have a dropped father, bowled daughter, which I've got nothing but stick for ever since." (2015)

The Keeling family fielded an all-Keeling team for the first time in their annual August Bank Holiday fixture against Sedlescombe in Sussex. They had previously come agonisingly close and reached ten but had to field one cousin with a different name. This time four brothers and their seven sons, aged between 59 and 18, not merely achieved their ambition but won the match. The game is the legacy of Sir John Keeling, who first mustered a family-led team to take on the village before the war; it has been held regularly since its resumption in 1965. "I'm one of eight brothers so there are quite a lot of first cousins lurking about," said captain Paul Keeling. (2016)

New Zealand's Broadcasting Standards Authority ordered a radio station to pay $NZ8,000 compensation to Ben Stokes's mother Deborah. Mrs Stokes had rung Radio Hauraki to complain about comments made about her son's infamous final over in the World Twenty20 final and found herself talking to presenter Matt Heath, who omitted to mention that they were live on air. (2016)

SLOW DAYS

The match between Marsden and South Hetton in the Durham Coast League was left drawn after Marsden batted throughout the allotted five hours, scored 136 for six, and then left. One batsman, Tony Shields, scored four not out in 187 minutes. South Hetton captain Bobby Steel had insisted on Marsden batting first because he said their captain, Colin Marshall, had not spun the coin within the required time. (1994)

Istabraque Shaikh, a 15-year-old fan of Rahul Dravid, scored 36 in four hours and twelve minutes in a three-day schools match in Mumbai. He was lbw just before the close of the first day. "Take it from me, we haven't shouted that loud an appeal in a long, long time," said bowler Salman Charolia. Two years earlier, Istabraque spent twelve and a half hours making 69 in a similar fixture. (2007)

Ten-year-old Trent Williams batted for 39.3 overs of a forty-over Under-16 match – and scored just one. Playing for Nursery Ridge in the Red Cliffs Cricket Association in Victoria, he came in at No. 3 to face the fourth ball of the innings and stayed there. The team finished on 44 for nine. (2007)

SMALL NUMBERS

In Yorkshire, NEACO, a team from an aluminium fencing works, were bowled out for four by the Railway Tavern in the Malton Pub and Works Evening League. However, NEACO won the game because their opponents had broken the league's registration rules. (1993)

Burton Latimer beat Weldon in the Corby & District Under-15 League without scoring a run off the bat. Weldon were all out for three in 5.4 overs, with Jeremy Nicholls and Carl Davidson taking five wickets each, then conceded four wides in the first over they bowled. (1994)

West Wight Middle School on the Isle of Wight were bowled out for nought, chasing Ryde School's 162 for no wicket. The Ryde cricket master, Chris Ody, said: "The West Wight boys performed in a dignified and sporting manner." (1997)

An Under-13 team from the Baranagar Ramakrishna Mission, batting one man short, were bowled out for nought by the Bournvita team in a match between rival cricket coaching centres in Calcutta. The innings lasted just eighteen minutes. Sayak Ghosh took six of the wickets, including a hat-trick, then hit the winning boundary from the second ball. (1998)

Petworth Park were bowled out for four by Burgess Hill in the Sussex Invitation League after half their team went home convinced the match would be abandoned. They were a man short anyway, and five more left at tea when it was raining heavily. "It was really a breakdown of communication," said Petworth player Jerry Wakeford. (1999)

Ten members of the Fareham & Crofton Fourth Eleven made ducks in the Hampshire Combination League fixture against Emsworth. The side were bowled out for 11, with captain Steve Godwin carrying his bat for eight not out; the other three runs were extras. Emsworth bowler Andy Philpot took eight for three. The ten batsmen were all teenagers. "We sat down afterwards and laughed it off as one of those days," said Godwin. (1999)

None of the eleven players in the Cuddalore women's team scored a run against Chennai Second Eleven in India. However, the side scraped to six all out – in reply to 158 for one declared – because of wides. One batter, Balasoundari, almost hit a four but the ball just failed to reach the boundary and she was unable to run because of cramp. (2000)

Victorian side Moorooduc, known as "The Ducs", were bowled out for ten in the Mornington Peninsula competition match against Tootgarook, and six of the Ducs scored ducks. (2001)

The Chacombe village team in Northamptonshire failed to score a single run between them in their opening fixture of the season, against Marston St Lawrence Second Eleven. They were bowled out for three, thanks to two wides and a bye. "Our side was all lads of 16 or 17," said former secretary Ted Garrett, "and they must have felt rotten. Some people will laugh at them but, in these couch-potato days, they should be applauded for turning out to keep village cricket alive." (2002)

Goldsborough Second Eleven failed to score a single run between them in a Nidderdale League match against Dishforth in North Yorkshire. The first ten batsmen were all caught for nought, and the team were all out for five, thanks only to four byes and a leg-bye. Gavin Hardisty took seven for nought. "We could have got a run," said Goldsborough captain Peter Horsman, "but the batsman had just been hit on the foot the ball before and he turned down the chance." (2006)

In reply to Banstead's 366 for eight in a Surrey League Division Three match, Hook & Southborough were bowled out for three. They were all out in twenty-three balls, batting three men short. (2008)

Newbury Under-11s had a total of 50 in their match against Mortimer West End – but none of their batsmen scored a run. Nine were bowled for ducks, and the tenth was run out. Their runs came from six no-balls and 19 wides, which all counted double under age-group rules. West End won by ten wickets. (2009)

In Sri Lanka, the Under-13 cricketers of Mayadunne Vidyalaya were bowled out for 15 and four in a two-innings match against Rajasinghe School. Kasun Heshan took 13 wickets. (2009)

Barrington were bowled out for six by Huish & Langport in Somerset League Division Two. They had safely reached three for nought, but then eight batsmen fell for ducks in reply to their opponents' 195 for seven. Huish & Langport captain Dominic Shillabeer took seven for two. (2012)

Sydney High were bowled out for nought by King's School in a Fourth Eleven match, with King's bowler Brad Thomas taking six wickets, his victims forming two separate hat-tricks. King's hit the winning run off a dropped sitter first ball. The sides then split into two scratch teams and played a far more satisfying Twenty20 fixture. (2012)

Nadeem Akhtar began his career as captain of Ellerslie Second Eleven in extraordinary fashion. His team bowled out Southwell Seconds for 22 in the South Notts League Division E, and knocked off the runs in nine balls. (2013)

Haslington bowled Wirral out for three in the Cheshire League, which represented a recovery from none for eight. Only the last man, Connor Hobson, scored a run off the bat, leaving Ben Istead with figures of six for one. Wirral had been chasing 109 to win. Matt Garrett, who came in at No. 9, said: "The reaction in the back of your mind is, 'I think we can still do this.' But two balls later, when you're following all your team-mates back to the clubhouse, you think perhaps it's not your day." (2014)

Pak Pakhtoon followed Wirral by being bowled out for three, the lowest total in the 121-year history of the Birmingham League. Jhalid Sadiq, opening the bowling for their opponents, Pioneers, finished with 7–5–2–7, including the no-ball that made up a third of the total. Two weeks earlier, Pak Pakhtoon had scored 300, largely thanks to 199 from Amsal

Zubair; this time he made one of eight ducks. Jubilant Pioneers batsman Imran Majid said: "When we rang the league, they didn't believe us. We had to take the scorecard around to the chairman." (2014)

Bapchild Cricket Club, from Kent, were bowled out for nought in 20 balls in a six-a-side indoor match (no not-out batsman) against Canterbury Christ Church University. "All they needed to do was hit a wall to get one run," said opponent Mike Rose. (2016)

SPIRIT OF CRICKET

A cricket club calling themselves the friendliest in England has emerged from Quad, an arts centre in Derby. Quad's chief executive, Adam Buss, wanted to return to the game after a long absence and, having found himself outclassed in other teams, sought "the reinvigoration of social cricket" and invited others to join him, saying "ability is no issue". Although Quad unexpectedly won their opening game, they have mostly lived up to their motto: *fervidus sed vacuus* (keen but useless). (2014) *Quad still appeared to be functioning in 2017 with the mission statement: "On a relentless quest to be the friendliest cricket team in the world."*

For the second year running, there was a tie in the annual St Columbanus parish match between the Curate's Eleven and the Rector's Eleven in Ballyholme, Northern Ireland. Both teams were bowled out for 45. Although the Rector's team claimed an extra run, it was agreed "in the spirit of the match" that a tie was the right result. (2014)

Bryn Darbyshire, playing for Lymington Second Eleven against South Wilts, was given out "handled the ball" after he threw it back to the bowler; no-ball had been called and he had hit it only a few inches. The dismissal led to a Lymington collapse and a 58-run defeat. Darbyshire admitted the umpire was probably right, but accused the opposition of bad sports-manship for appealing: "I had hit the same bowler for six off my second ball and was taking him apart. They probably wanted to see the back of me." (2015)

A Harris Shield match between two Mumbai schools turned to farce after 14-year-old left-arm spinner Daksh Agarwal of Vibgyor High took the first nine wickets against St Joseph's Secondary. With the last pair still 71 short, Agarwal's team-mates devoted themselves to ensuring he got all ten. Their efforts included the wicketkeeper standing with the ball by the stumps as the batsmen ran nine, and intentionally bad bowling from the other end. Finally, Agarwal ended the nonsense by effecting a run-out off his own bowling for a 51-run win. "I am not disappointed," he said. "I have an all-ten. My team won. So what if my tenth wicket is a run-out? I am proud." (2015)

Kingsville Baptist Cricket Club lost their chance of reaching the semi-finals of their Victorian Turf Cricket Association tournament when the pitch was vandalised. They arrived for the second day of their match against Sunshine strongly placed to win and finish in the top four – only to find the pitch had been dug up and covered with oil. No alternative pitch could be found and Kingsville missed qualification by two points. With Sunshine out of the running, suspicion fell on the other contending teams. "It would be hugely disappointing to find out it is someone from the cricket family," said Cricket Victoria chief executive Tony Dodemaide, "but that is the direction it is pointing at the moment." (2016)

An outfielder deliberately kicked a stationary ball over the boundary to prevent the batsmen running three, thus keeping a tailender on strike for the next over. The incident happened when Prahran were battling to save a Premier League game against Melbourne. Cricket Victoria said they would take no action but wrote to Melbourne reminding them of the "spirit of cricket". (2017)

Former Pakistan captain Javed Miandad, 59, said match-fixers should be executed. "Why don't you take strong measures? You should give death penalty to such people. We must not tolerate such things, not at all," Miandad said. He was supported by his former team-mate Abdul Qadir, who said that if players involved previously had been hanged, the practice would have stopped. (2017)

TIMES CHANGE (EXCEPT WHEN THEY DON'T)

A Hambledon ladies' team has played its first match at Broadhalfpenny Down, where the modern game developed. "After 250 years it was time the village had a ladies' team of its own," said the opening batsman, Marina Steel. (1999)

The Graces, Britain's first openly homosexual team, have applied to join the Surrey Cricket Board. The side includes former Yorkshire League and Minor County players. "People think we're just a load of old queens who think we look good in white, but actually we can and do play well," said captain Ian Crossland. "Sport is one of the last bastions of male homophobia." One of WG's great-granddaughters, Rosemary Douglas, complained: "They are cashing in on the Grace name and it is unsuitable for this team to do so." (2000)

An 11-year-old girl, Bethany Brown, playing for Monk Bretton in a junior cup-tie in Yorkshire, stunned the all-male opposition of Elsecar by taking seven for nought in three overs. She took four in four balls in her last over. (2000)

Bengali film-maker Anjaan Chaudhury offered a film role to Donna Ganguly, wife of Indian captain Sourav, as a dancer in his forthcoming film, *Chandramallika*. When Ganguly would not allow his wife to act opposite any other male artiste, Chaudhury agreed to cast him as well. (2000)

The tradition of friendly games during intervals at the Adelaide Oval has been ended because of insurance costs. Ball games – even catch – are to be banned. In January, a woman spectator had her eyesight permanently damaged after being hit. (2002)

The newest status symbols at the Sydney Ashes Test were "beer wenches", girls wearing hot pants and tight T-shirts hired for $A65 an hour to fetch the beers for groups of (male) spectators. "It's not too bad for the girls, they do get jostled and harassed a bit, but there are worse ways to spend your day," said a spokesman for their agency, Sex Bomb Promotions. (2003)

Police have clamped down on the SCG's beer wenches despite their popularity. Inspector Mark Szalajko yesterday said they promoted irresponsible drinking: "So far this week we have ejected four of them, all for serving alcohol to intoxicated persons, and one lady for acting in an offensive manner. My message to potential beer wenches is 'Stay home or face fines of up to $550.'" (2004)

Two women umpires took charge of a first-team Bolton League match for the first time. Karen Knott and Gail Ashton umpired Farnworth v Heaton. (2004)

New Zealand Cricket threatened to eject two women for kissing at a one-day international against Sri Lanka in Napier. A security guard moved in to stop the women after the kiss, which was caught by the TV cameras. Mother of three Richelle Holloway, 29, was at the match with Kelly Holdway, 20 – and her boyfriend. New Zealand Cricket marketing manager Peter Dwan said the kiss was part of "an ongoing display" by the pair, who had been dancing beforehand: "The judgment of the security guard had nothing to do with morality or sexuality but related to the safety of the crowd," Mr Dwan said. (2006)

Following Darren Gough's success in winning the TV contest *Strictly Come Dancing* in 2005, Essex have decided to incorporate dance steps into their pre-season warm-ups. "Goughie lost a stone in weight and built up so much leg strength because of the dancing," captain Ronnie Irani said. "I think it could benefit us all greatly." (2006)

ECB officials intervened to stop Liverpool & District Competition club Southport Trinity being sponsored by a chain of sex shops. The club had agreed a deal whereby the players' shirts would have the logo and web address of the Nice'n'Naughty chain. The club were told they would be docked all points accrued while wearing the shirts. "We didn't realise it would cause this much of a problem," said club chairman Colin Maxwell. "We are living in 2006." (2006)

Giles Clarke, the Somerset chairman, complained to the ECB after receiving what was described as a sexist text message from his Leicestershire counterpart, Neil Davidson. After his team had won a Pro40 match between the counties Davidson allegedly texted Clarke: "I can see why Somerset is the home of girls' cricket." (2006)

Shane Warne is the hero of Australia's young males, according to Paul Merrill, editor of the country's top-selling lads' mag, *Zoo*. "He's supposedly shagged a thousand women, he's fat, he smokes and he drinks beer." (2006)

The Otago Cricket Association apologised to the West Indies for using the slogan "It's all white here" to promote the New Zealand v West Indies Test in Dunedin. "We just wanted a catchy phrase to help sell the game," said chief executive Ross Dykes. "It was all based around the association of the colour with cricket." (2008)

In Pakistan, a team of eunuchs beat a team of "normal" male cricketers in what is thought to have been the first match of its kind. The Sanam (Beloved) Eleven easily beat a local club, the Olympians, before a large crowd in the city of Sukkur. Eunuchs have long been regarded as outcasts in Pakistan – earning a precarious living by dancing, begging or prostitution – but Pakistan's chief justice, Iftikhar Chaudhry, has been working hard to improve the eunuchs' status. After the players had done an impromptu celebratory dance, captain Sanam Khan dedicated the victory to Justice Chaudhry. (2009)

England fast bowler Jimmy Anderson has posed naked (though not full-frontally) for gay magazine *Attitude*. Anderson, who is married, said he did not believe there was homophobia in cricket. Asked how he would respond if a cricketer came out, he said: "I'd throw them a special gay cricket tea." (2010)

The village cricket club at Slaithwaite, Yorkshire, was persuaded to take down adverts of a bikini-clad model near the local railway station after residents complained of sexism. The signs showed Lara Bingle, Michael Clarke's one-time fiancée, holding a bat, and were designed to entice visitors following the "Ale Trail" to go to the clubhouse. The club's joint-president, Tim Garside, said they had also put up versions showing men in swimming trunks, "so I don't think it's sexist at all". (2014)

The captain's wife rescued Ushaw Moor Second Eleven when the team were several men short for a Durham League fixture at Shildon Railway. Darren Gill's wife Deborah, an experienced cricketer herself, was drafted in and hit the winning boundary. "To be honest, this is probably the only time she's going to get picked," said her husband afterwards. (2014)

Street cricket has become the latest battleground for a growing women's rights movement in Pakistan. Women and girls are posting photos of themselves taking part in traditionally male pursuits such as cricket, hanging out at the beach, climbing trees and eating in roadside cafes known as *dhabas*. "Most of us could narrate instances of childhood where we were either told by the boys playing street cricket that we can't play with them or were discouraged or not allowed by parents," said Sadia Khatri, one of the movement's founders. "Cricket on the streets is something girls aren't supposed to do, so it seemed like a natural next step to take." (2015)

The former New Zealand cricketer Danny Morrison wore a red turban and fake beard when he oversaw the toss as a commentator in an IPL match in the majority-Sikh city of Mohali. The stunt was widely criticised as insulting, but Morrison insisted he was asked to dress up by the broadcasters, Sony TV. And the president of the New Zealand Indian Cricket Association, Bhikhu Bhana, was supportive: "Cricket can open bridges really and I think Danny tries to do it sometimes. Look at the crowds there. They're having a good time. From my point of view, I can see nothing culturally offensive from Danny Morrison." (2016)

Among the questions in a PE theory exam at a high school in Bhiwindi, Maharashtra, was "What is Virat Kohli's girlfriend's name?" (2016)

The Queer Premier League (QPL), a tournament organised by a lesbian support group in advance of the annual Mumbai Pride march, has been played for the third time, with eighty players taking part from the LGBTQ+ community in the city. One cheerleader, Sumit, said: "It's especially fun because for once we have women playing on the pitch and men cheerleading." (2017)

Storms that hit Britain in December 2015 caused more than £3.5 million worth of damage at 57 cricket clubs, according to an ECB report. Professor Piers Forster, a meteorologist at Leeds University, said: "UK weather will always bowl us the odd googly, but climate change is making them harder to defend against." (2017)

New research into traditional crafts sponsored by the Radcliffe Trust lists cricket ball-making as one of four crafts that has now become extinct in Britain along with gold-beating, sieve- and riddle-making and lacrosse-stick-making. "Today, no one manufactures hand-stitched cricket balls in the UK," according to the Radcliffe Red List. "In some cases, the raw materials are sent from the UK to the Indian subcontinent for fabrication, and the balls are then finished in the UK." Cricket bat-making is listed as "endangered" but not "critically endangered". (2017)

MCC and the Royal Academy of Dance have launched a pilot scheme in primary schools trying to encourage more boys to try ballet and girls to try cricket. Alexander Campbell, the Royal Ballet's cricket-loving principal dancer, is acting as the academy's ambassador for the project. (2017)

The BCCI has banned Dharamveer Pal, who is partially paralysed by polio, from working as a ballboy and has issued an instruction that no other physically handicapped people are to be employed in the role. This followed criticism on social media. "Poor advertisement for polio-free India," said one tweet. "I have been cheering the Indian team for years now and will continue to do so," said Dharamaveer, who has "Cricket is the reason for my living" tattooed on his arm." (2017)

A racist flyer attacking Indian and Chinese-origin electoral candidates has been distributed in Edison, New Jersey. "The Chinese and Indians are taking over our town. Chinese school! Indian school! Cricket fields! Enough is enough", the flyer said. Next to their pictures was the word "Deport". The two targets, Jerry Shi and Falguni Patel, both won. (2017)

TRAGEDY

Five people were electrocuted after a man in Negombo, Sri Lanka, tried to put up a 42-foot booster aerial to watch the Singer World Series cricket. P. D. Appuhamy, 40, and his wife were killed when the piping containing the antenna fell on an electrical cable. Three neighbours, including two 16-year-old boys, who tried to extricate them were also killed. (1996)

A 20-year-old man poisoned himself in southern Sri Lanka after being scolded by his mother for playing too much cricket. Visantha Kumara left a note saying he was "sacrificing his life for the game of cricket" and asked that he be buried with a bat and ball in his coffin so he should be a better cricketer when he is reborn. (1997)

A 13-year-old boy, Chanminoa Panagodage, fell three storeys to his death in Colombo after he climbed up the outside of a school building to get a piece of wood to use as a cricket bat. Pupils had been banned from bringing bats to school. (1998)

A 26-year-old Rawalpindi man was allegedly shot dead by his uncle for supporting India against Pakistan in a one-day international. Muzaffar Ahmed died in hospital of his wounds. His uncle, Arbab Ahmed, was arrested. "It is a sad incident," said the officer in charge of the case, "but it proves how much people love their country and the national cricket team." (1998)

An inquest delivered a verdict of accidental death after being told that Gordon Bryden, a hospital consultant, had died in the wake of a collision with a team-mate as they attempted to take the same catch. Dr Bryden was detained in hospital for three weeks after the accident, which occurred in June while he was playing for the Sheffield club Parkhead against Youlgreave. He was readmitted when his condition deteriorated, and later suffered a fatal haemorrhage. William Thomas, a consultant surgeon, likened the injury to those suffered by victims of car crashes. (2002)

Progress on the controversial Rangiri Dambulla Stadium in Kandy was interrupted when one worker fell to his death and another was seriously injured. Makeshift scaffolding and strong winds were blamed. (2002)

Richard Smith, 29, of Queensbury Cricket Club, in West Yorkshire, collapsed and died during a Halifax League game after hitting eight sixes in an innings of 98 against Bridgeholme. His father, David, had suffered the same fate 18 years earlier while bowling. (2003)

Schoolboy cricketers in Gazipur, northern Bangladesh, battered a teammate to death after he accidentally smashed a newly won trophy. Identified solely as Rajiv, the teenager was waving the cup with one hand when it dropped on the pavement, whereupon fellow team members set about him with sticks. (2003)

A bolt of lightning killed a cricketer with a shock so intense it shattered his bat. David Evans was playing for the Bomaderry Fourth Grade team in southern New South Wales when the bolt hit out of a clear sky. "The bat just exploded," said Bomaderry secretary Graeme Sawkins. "It left a hole in the ground next to the wicket where he was standing and six or seven other players got knocked down with the impact." Evans, 31, came from a well-known local cricketing family. (2004)

Richard Lightwood died while playing cricket, just as his twin brother did twelve years earlier. Richard, 27, collapsed while bowling for Kings Bromley, Staffordshire, against Uttoxeter Second Eleven at 1.20pm on Saturday. He had watched in 1994 when his brother Andrew dropped dead while batting for Lichfield Under-15s, also at 1.20pm. Both boys had a heart condition but were fit and athletic. "I believe they are together now," said their mother Angela. "That is the only thing keeping me going." (2006)

Aas Mohammed, playing cricket at Ghaziabad, Haryana, was killed when he fell into a 12-foot-deep sewer tank that had been left open. (2007)

Mehmood Ali, 18, was shot dead by a security guard in Lahore after being warned not to play cricket near the airport. (2007)

A 37-year-old father, Dean Harrison, was killed when his motorcycle collided with a van and he was hurled on to the outfield of Stone Cricket Club in Worcestershire where a match was taking place against Droitwich Third Eleven. Retired fireman Peter Harler, who was batting, tried unsuccessfully to revive him. (2008)

One man died and another was seriously injured after they waded into the surf to fetch the ball during a game of beach cricket at Lake Tyers, Victoria. Police said they were carried away by a rip on a dangerous stretch of shore. (2009)

Mohammed Junaid Hussain, 17, died in hospital after being struck by lightning while sheltering under a tree with friends. They had all been playing cricket in Small Heath Park, Birmingham, when the storm started. Five of the other players were also detained in hospital. (2009)

Mohammad Qureshi was watching friends play cricket while perched on the parapet wall of his apartment in Ahmedabad when he dived to catch a soaring hit and plunged to his death. (2001)

A lethal batch of home-made liquor sold at a cricket match has killed at least thirty-one people near Lucknow, with more than a hundred others ill in hospital, according to police and medical officials. A suspect has been arrested. Such incidents are not uncommon in India: in 2011, 170 people died in West Bengal from drinking moonshine. (2015)

Two boys, aged 16 and 11, were electrocuted and six others injured inside a tent being used as a commentary box at a match near Jamnagar in

Gujarat. Police said it appeared that organisers had illegally tapped into the main power line and that the current had passed through the metal in the tent. (2016)

A 16-year-old boy in Ambalangoda, Sri Lanka, hanged himself after his parents refused him permission to attend a cricket match, saying he needed to study. (2016)

TURF

Lash Dem Lara, a three-year-old roan colt named after Brian Lara, won the Trinidad Derby in record time. The horse was bred, owned and trained by members of the Hadeed family who, like Lara, were educated at Fatima College. (1994)

Shane Warne, a four-year-old bay colt, beat eleven rivals to win the Pakistan Derby, the country's richest horse race, at Lahore. (1996)

Jack Hobbs, trained by John Gosden, won the Irish Derby by five lengths, having finished runner-up in the Epsom Derby. Racing historian John Randall said the colt joined a list of successful horses named after cricketers. These included: Don Bradman, who won two races over the Grand National fences in 1936 (though not the National itself); Intikhab, officially rated the best horse in Europe in 1998 after romping home in the Queen Anne Stakes at Royal Ascot; Tendulkar, third in the 2001 Dewhurst Stakes at Newmarket; Flintoff, who was jointly owned by the eponymous Andrew when runner-up in the 2009 Midlands Grand

National; Warne, winner of the 2014 Fox Hunters' Chase at Aintree; and Bishan Bedi, a son of Intikhab, who has been winning races at Dundalk for trainer Aidan O'Brien. (2015) *Randall understandably overlooked the fate of another Irish-bred son of Intikhab, Wisden. He ran once at Wolverhampton in 2015, came eighth out of ten, was gelded and sold to run in Bahrain. "Such a disappointment with all his issues," said a spokeswoman for trainer Sir Michael Stoute.*

UMPIRES

Bishop Auckland's West Indian professional Ricky Waldren was caught on the boundary when the ball ricocheted off the head of the umpire at the bowler's end, George Simpson. He needed ten stitches. "Luckily, these ex-miners are made of strong stuff," said Bishop Auckland chairman Keith Hopper. "George went to hospital but got back to the bar for last orders." (1995)

Brian Robinson, 74, an umpire in the North Lancashire & Cumbria League, claimed he was a victim of discrimination after being asked to resign because of his epilepsy. An umpires' federation official, Colin Bickerstaffe, said epilepsy was only one reason for the decision: "It is just that the committee felt he was no longer up to the rigours of umpiring." After a strongly worded letter from the British Epilepsy Association and a threat of legal action under disability discrimination laws, Robinson was reinstated. (2000)

The Northern Premier League fixture between Darwen and Lancaster was abandoned because no umpires turned up. Ken Shenton, secretary of the umpires' federation, said it was a protest against the teams' poor disciplinary record. (2003)

An umpire in a schools match in Colombo was reported to the local cricket authorities for calling his fiancée on his mobile while officiating. Players complained he had completely ignored an appeal when he was on the phone. (2007)

In Bermuda, the Premier League match between Devonshire and Willow Cuts was abandoned when both umpires walked off the field, separately, after suffering verbal abuse. Bobby Smith had already gone after Cuts players and spectators had bombarded him with obscenities following a controversial decision. Cuts batsman Chris Douglas then came out to replace him; the remaining umpire Lester Harnett decided to call off the match anyway, whereupon would-be umpire Douglas kicked over the stumps before storming off himself. (2011)

Charles Fenton, 92, and believed to be the oldest umpire in Britain, may be able to continue in the job in 2013 after all. He was originally forced to announce his retirement after 61 years officiating in the Derbyshire & Cheshire League because insurers refused to provide cover for anyone over 85 without an extra premium. However, publicity-minded book-makers Paddy Power offered to pay the extra. "What kind of skipper declares with his batsman on 92?" said a spokesman. (2012) *Later reports said Fenton did retire after all, but was given a special community award from the Hyde Rotary Club – and the publicity surrounding the case turned him into a local celebrity. He had sort-of come to terms with retirement:*

"It was ridiculous why I had to stop umpiring but I suppose it's time for a break…"

The life-size statue of umpire Dickie Bird in his home town of Barnsley has been placed on a higher plinth, five feet off the ground, to stop revellers hanging items from his raised finger. Decorations have included condoms, bras and knickers, and Bird has been spotted removing them himself. Sculptor Graham Ibbeson said it was impossible to stop such incidents: "What we are going to do is make it a little more difficult." Bird said his only concern was that someone might get hurt. (2013)

UNSAYABLE

Denise Annetts, who has won thirteen Test caps, claimed she had been omitted from the Australian national women's team because she was not a lesbian. Her complaint was rejected by the selectors, who said she had lost form, and by Australia's Anti-Discrimination Board, which said it was illegal to discriminate against homosexuals but not heterosexuals. (1994)

The Duke of Edinburgh was attacked as "stupid" and "insensitive" by people campaigning for gun control in the wake of the Dunblane primary school massacre when he compared guns to cricket bats. He said on BBC Radio: "If a cricketer, for instance, suddenly decided to go into a school

and batter a lot of people to death with a cricket bat, which he could do very easily. I mean, are you going to ban cricket bats?" (1996)

Australia's Anti-Discrimination Board reported that Britons complained of racial abuse more than any other ethnic group in the country, and said the level of complaints rose during England cricket tours. Chris Puplick, the board chairman, said expatriates were often upset by TV commentators saying that Poms would play better cricket if they washed more. He added that most complaints were unjustified, and indicated hypersensitivity rather than racial hatred. (1997)

Gay and lesbian groups demanded an apology after American comedian Jerry Lewis, 82, called cricket a "fag game" at a press conference in Sydney. Lewis then mimed an effeminate gesture holding an imaginary cricket bat. (2008)

Actor Jason Alexander, best known for playing George in *Seinfeld*, posted a thousand-word apology after repeatedly calling cricket "a gay sport" on an American chat show. Some of his followers on Twitter had told him they were both gay and offended. There were no reports of complaints from cricketers. (2012)

The West Indian batsman Chris Gayle asked an Australian TV news reporter for a date while being interviewed live on air. After scoring 41 off 15 balls for Melbourne Renegades in the Big Bash League he told Network Ten journalist Mel McLaughlin that he had played well just so she would interview him. "Your eyes are beautiful, hopefully we can win this game and then we can have a drink after as well," Gayle told her. "Don't blush, baby." A chorus of anger was led by McLaughlin, who said female sports journalists should be treated as professionals: "We want equality, we always want equality," she said. Gayle said later: "It was just a joke." (2016)

Geoffrey Boycott apologised for an insulting remark at a Q&A session during the Edgbaston Test against West Indies. He told guests that knighthoods had been showered on West Indian cricketers "like confetti", adding: "Mine's been turned down twice. I'd better black me face."(2017)

VIRTUALLY IMPOSSIBLE

Lymington Second Eleven tied three successive matches in Division One of the Hampshire League. First, they matched 177 by Winchester KS Second Eleven; the following week, Tim Hunter hit 17 off the final over to equal Penton's 274 for five; then they batted first, scoring 167 for nine against Sparsholt, who were all out off the final ball – for 167. (1998)

Matt Garnaut and Bret Mulder put on 177 for the last wicket at the WACA ground in Perth to give Bayswater-Morley victory over Midland-Guildford in the final of the Perth first-grade competition. Garnaut scored a maiden century, 127 not out. Mulder, aged 35, made an unbeaten 70, having played nineteen seasons in the league without scoring a fifty. "Initially I thought I'd have a slog," said Garnaut, "then as the target got closer, I decided to play straight." "I feel as though I've just been through a war," said defeated captain Mark Lavender. (1999)

Mark Tomlinson scored an all-run eight for Valley End against Croydon Gas in Surrey. The bowler and all the fielders left a straight drive to each other and the ball stopped a foot short of the boundary. (1999)

Jeremy Henderson, a former captain of Harrogate Cricket Club, played in three tied matches in three days over the Bank Holiday weekend. He was involved in two Second Eleven league matches for the club, against Clifton Alliance and Osbaldwick on the Saturday and the Monday, both of which ended in a tie. And on the Sunday he turned out for Hampsthwaite in a friendly against Harrogate Squash Club, which was also tied. "I've been playing league cricket since 1967 and must have played about a thousand games," he said. "In all that time, I can probably

only recall two tied games before. The odds must be astronomical."
(1999)

A flying bail landed on the pavilion roof at Market Deeping, Lincolnshire. Mark Pilgrim of Billingborough was bowled by 16-year-old Mark Stanway when the bail flew fifty yards, hit the roof and slid down into the guttering. Stanway was described as "quite quick" and the weather "a bit breezy", but Market Deeping captain Nick Andrews said: "You couldn't do it again if you tried. It was just one of those freak incidents." (2006)

Aberdeenshire team Methlick, needing 19 off the final ball to win a seven-a-side match against Fraserburgh, tied the game. Fifteen-year-old bowler Peter Clark bowled two no-balls, both hit for six by Colin Addison. His third ball was fair, and Addison only managed a four. "Peter's a fine young player," said Fraserburgh secretary Ian McCallum, "and he has a story he'll be able to tell for the rest of his life." (2006)

William Bell, who came to the crease when New Zealand team Karori were 27 for nine against the North City Trojans, hit a six off his first ball, 27 off his first over, and went on to make 100 not out. He shared a stand of 148 with Baz Taniwha, who was run out in the final over when he went over to congratulate Bell on his century. Karori won by 51 runs. Bell normally opens the batting but was late leaving work. (2008)

Lee Wood and Toby Harper shared a century opening stand for Hartley Wintney in the club's traditional bank holiday fixture against a team fielded by Harlequins rugby club. Of the first hundred, Wood scored 93, Extras seven – and Harper nought. Harper had allowed his partner, known as a swashbuckler, to farm the strike. Then, after Wood retired on scoring his century, he stayed to reach double figures. "Toby got by far the biggest cheer of the day — far louder than for Lee's hundred — when he finally scored a run," said Hartley Wintney committee member Jonathan Rowe. (2009)

Napier Technical Old Boys, New Zealand, lost their last four wickets off three balls against Napier Old Boys Marist. One batsman was stumped off a wide, the next was bowled first ball, and a third caught and bowled, giving off-spinner Indika Senerathne a hat-trick. The last remaining batsman, Craig Herrick, had been acting as scorer and was under-standably rather busy. By the time he reached the crease he was timed out. (2011)

Elton and Edgworth of the Bolton Association played each other at first-and second-team level on a Sunday in June, and both games were tied. In each case, the chasing team needed two off the last ball, but could manage only a single. (2012)

Jason Hughes returned to Sydney grade cricket with Mosman three weeks after the death of his younger brother Phillip, the Australian Test player, and was out for 63, the score Phillip had reached when he was fatally struck. Jason said he had not known how many runs he had when he was dismissed. (2014)

Shania-Lee Swart hit a match-winning 160 while her team-mates contributed no runs between them. Swart's team made 169 for nine for Mpumalanga Under-19s in their Twenty20 match against Easterns at a tournament in Pretoria, but the other nine all came from extras. Swart hit 18 fours and 12 sixes. (2016)

Freddy Walker scored an unbeaten 150 off 125 balls batting No. 11 for Hamilton against Bay of Plenty. Walker came in at 189 for nine and shared an unbroken 220-run partnership with the No. 3, Anish Desai. Walker had scored just 54 in six previous innings over three seasons in the competition, which is just below first-class. "They were a little bit unlucky," he said, "but we were due a bit of luck too, and we got it." (2017)

Moonee Valley batsman Jatinder Singh's middle stump was sent flying but the bails remained in place. The incident happened in a match against Strathmore Heights in Melbourne and made everyone scratch their heads about how it happened, which remained mysterious, and what the umpire's decision should be. Singh was eventually given out, which was apparently correct under what was then Law 28: "The wicket is put down if a bail is completely removed from the top of the stumps, or a stump is struck out of the ground." Another Australian, Jacobi Unbehaun, was also given out when a similar incident took place in an Under-17 match in

Geraldton, but in this case the decision was thought to be wrong, as the stump remained in the ground. (2017)

Needing 35, Dorchester-on-Thames scored 40 off the final over to win their Oxfordshire Cricket Association match against Swinbrook. Steve McComb, who says he prefers to hit boundaries due to an arthritic ankle, hit 6, 6, 0, 4, 4, 6, 6, 6 off Mihai Cucos. There were two no-balls. (2017)

WE CAN DO ANYTHING

Teenager Mark Tomlinson agreed to play for Glazebury Second Eleven, near Warrington, against Rylands until 4.30pm when he had to leave for the airport to fly off on holiday with his parents. He took four for 44 as the opposition were bowled out for 67, then hit an unbeaten 51 to win the game. Luckily, his home adjoined the ground, and he leapt back over the garden fence with a minute to spare. (1998)

Garnet White, a 21-year-old Jamaican making his debut for Parley Second Eleven against Puddletown in the Dorset League, hit 173 not out then took eight for one, all bowled. Ian Belt, the opposing captain, described the experience as "pretty terrifying". (2001)

Australian Cameron Nupier took all ten wickets and scored a century for Hornchurch against Shenfield in the Essex Premier Division. Nupier made 114 out of 258 for eight declared, then had figures of 17–1–42–10 in a 142-run win. (2007)

Mark O'Brien of Broadmeadows Third Eleven had figures of 13–11–3–8, bowling Sunshine out for 71 in a Victorian sub-district match. O'Brien then hit 112 not out on the way to an innings victory. (2010)

Kirstan Kallicharan, Trinidad & Tobago's Under-15 captain, scored 404 not out in an Under-14 match for Vishnu Boys against Valencia, with 44 fours and 31 sixes. Vishnu made 548 for one in their 35 overs, and Valencia were out for 89, with Kallicharan taking two for none with his leg-spin. (2014)

WELL FIELDED!

Joshua Wiles, 12, achieved a hat-trick of run-outs off the last three balls of a South Australia schools match. He was playing for St John's Lutheran Primary School junior A-grade team against Mitcham Primary, who needed five to win with three balls left. The match was left drawn. (1999)

Seam bowler Gavin Bailiff took a hat-trick for Bashley Second Eleven against Paultons in the Southern Premier League, all of them caught by John Childs. He took the first two at cover, and the third at midwicket to a left-hander. (2008)

Michael Morton, 28, became the first spectator to win the $NZ100,000 (about £50,000) brewery-sponsored prize for catching a six one-handed at a one-day international in New Zealand. Morton was sitting with his father on the bank at Seddon Park, Hamilton, when West Indies batsman Kieran Powell smashed the ball in his direction. Morton stood up after his dad yelled his name. "It sailed straight in to my hand," he said. (2014)

Tax consultant Ollie Newton, aiming for the same $100,000 prize as Michael Morton a few days earlier, was disqualified because he was not wearing the correct clothes. To be eligible, spectators had to wear the Tui brewery T-shirt; Newton was still in his suit, the T-shirts having all been sold by the time he arrived at the ground in Wellington. He caught the ball despite eating a plate of chips at the time. (2014)

WHAT DID YOU SAY STOPPED PLAY?

The Barbados League match between St John the Baptist and Police was halted when **Fidel Castro**, the President of Cuba and a former baseball player, stopped as he was being driven past the ground and asked if he could try the game. Castro, in his military uniform, faced three balls from a Police bowler and missed them all before thanking his hosts and leaving. (1994)

The match between Dominica and Grenada in the Windward Islands tournament at Windsor Park, Dominica, was abandoned midway through the final day when an **angry mob** protesting against an increase in motor licence fees invaded the field and uprooted the stumps. Protesters said their views were being ignored: the island's radio station was broadcasting the cricket. (1994)

The match between the South African Under-19 team and the Northern Transvaal Colts at the Correctional Services ground in Pretoria was reduced from 55 overs a side to 50 after the start was delayed because the stumps had been **stolen**. (1994)

Play in the village match against Cowling at Chatburn, Lancashire, was stopped because of the **noise** coming from a nearby field. The Chatburn wicketkeeper then realised the commotion was caused by a farmer chasing his dog, which was chasing a herd of cows. The wicket-keeper then angrily chased the farmer. What followed was described as "ten minutes of classic slapstick" before tempers cooled. Rodney Booth, the Chatburn captain, said the keeper then dropped three catches, which was probably responsible for his side's nine-run defeat. (1995)

A **boy falling out of a tree** stopped play in a Winchester Evening League match between the city's fire service and the rugby club. An outfielder heard 11-year-old Thomas Wainwright's screams after he had fallen thirty feet and become trapped in the lower branches. The firemen then formed a human chain to take him to safety. The boy suffered a dislocated leg; the fire brigade lost. (1995)

A match in Boddington, Gloucestershire, was abandoned because the pitch was engulfed by **smoke** from the Companion's Rest animal crematorium in nearby Elmstone Hardwicke. (1995)

Eight male streakers stopped play in the Pembrokeshire League match between Neyland and Lawrenny. They were believed to be guests at a nearby stag party. (1996)

In Lincolnshire, a friendly between Bardney and Horncastle was halted by a **hang-glider** which crashed into Horncastle fielder John Hague as he was running in to field a ball on the boundary. Hague received a glancing blow on the head. "I nearly didn't play because I'd woken up with a migraine," said Hague. "Being biffed on the head by a hang-glider was all I needed." The pilot said he had been trying to avoid a field of crops. The players helped him remove his broken glider before all of them, including Hague, carried on. (1997) The *Horncastle News* headlined the item "Bad Flight Stopped Play".

A Cornwall League Division One match between Helston and Falmouth was held up for ninety minutes after thousands of **bees** swarmed on to the ground. Two players were stung and bee specialists had to be called to collect the swarm before play could resume. (1997)

The Second Eleven match between Melksham and Bathford in Wiltshire was interrupted so that players could light bonfires to disperse an invasion of **flying ants**. In Cornwall, the match between Lanner and St Day was abandoned after a similar attack; an attempt to solve the problem by pouring boiling water on the ground proved unsuccessful. (1997)

A **bad smell** stopped play at Newlands, on the first day of the first-class match between Western Province and Free State. Players and umpires

raced off with shirts and jerseys pulled over their heads, and handker-
chiefs stuffed into their mouths. Western Province chief executive Arthur
Turner said: "It was a terrible, bad eggs, ammonia, kind of smell. It was
almost overpowering." A small explosion in the nearby brewery turned
out to be responsible. (1997)

Players from the Whitchurch club in Bristol abandoned their game
to chase two **burglars** they saw stealing a video recorder from a
nearby house. They eventually cornered the men in a nearby field.
(1997)

The **disgruntled parents** of a teenage boy stopped play at a school tournament to protest against his omission from the Tamil Nadu team. They
held up the start of the inter-state Under-14 tournament in Chennai for
nearly forty minutes by sitting on the pitch. "Injustice has been done to
my son Pramod Doss," said his father Deva Doss. "It surprises me how a
boy good enough to be in the Under-16 city squad cannot find a place in
the Under-14 state Eleven." They were finally persuaded to leave by officials. (1998)

A **magpie** stopped play at Ryde on the Isle of Wight. It swooped and
stole the keys from the ignition of a motorised roller which was about to
roll the pitch. The start was delayed until a tractor could tow the roller
away. (1998)

A **naked woman** drove across the outfield on a quad bike, stopping the
match between Hoveringham and the Inland Revenue in Nottinghamshire for more than five minutes. (1998)

Two police cars chasing a **drunken moped rider** across the outfield
stopped play in a Suffolk Premier League match. Deben Valley were
batting against the Ipswich & East Suffolk team at Woodbridge when the
rider appeared, waving at the police and taunting them. He eventually
fell off and was arrested. (1998)

Play was stopped in an Under-12 match at Maroubra, New South Wales,
by an **angry father** marching on to the field with a camcorder. He was
disputing a hit-wicket decision against his son. After everyone had

gathered round to watch the replay, the umpire agreed he had made a bad decision and rescinded it. (1999)

The First Eleven game at St Agnes in the Isles of Scilly against St Martin's had to be abandoned because a pair of **ringed plovers** had nested at square leg and produced four eggs. The club decided to scrap all home fixtures until the chicks had flown the nest. (1999)

Kent women, playing an Under-21 match against Sussex, refused to accept a **local rule** at Roedean School of "nought and out" for hits on to the A259 main road. The team said the rule hampered "flair and attacking strokemaking", and the game only started when their players were allowed to ignore it. "They said you can't have local rules," complained Terry Burton, the Sussex manager, "which is a bit rich coming from Kent where they have a local rule concerning the tree at Canterbury. I don't know why they made such a fuss because most of their girls couldn't get the ball off the square." Sussex won by 147 runs. (1999)

Players fled when a **goat** escaped from a field and charged them during a match between St John's and St Mary at Sevenoaks, Kent. (1999)

A Sri Lankan Tamil cricket festival in Southall, Middlesex, was halted on Bank Holiday Monday when rival groups of **Tamil gunmen** opened fire on each other outside the ground. About 3,000 spectators were watching a special exhibition game – in which Kris Srikkanth and Phil Simmons were guesting – when an armed policeman in a flak jacket walked on and told umpire David Webb to abandon the match. (1999)

Portugal's run-chase against the MCC in Vale do Lobo was interrupted when the computer-controlled undersoil **sprinkler system** suddenly came on and forced the players to flee to dry land. Portugal won by three wickets. (1999)

Downside, the Catholic school in Somerset, has modified its practice of ringing the **angelus bell** at six o'clock every evening, even during cricket matches. The players were always obliged to stop the game and turn towards the Abbey, an act of piety regarded by some rival schools as "a sneaky Papist plot" that disrupted matches at crucial moments. Now the angelus can be put back to 6.40 – after close of play. (2000)

A match played at Colchester Garrison had to be abandoned after the players were overwhelmed by **parachutists**. Marks Tey and Shalford were forced off the field by jumps being staged at a cocktail party for senior army officers and other dignitaries. The clubs had been warned in advance that there was a double booking, but they could not be told what the other event was for security reasons. (2000)

Amersham Second Eleven's Chiltern League fixture with Taplow was held up when a **sniper** with an air rifle opened fire on the players. "I had just taken a wicket and we were celebrating," explained the Taplow bowler Mike Bradley, felled after being hit in the leg by a pellet. "There was a whistling noise and it was like a real hard smack on the leg. It was quite a shock." A pellet flew just past the head of Amersham's Ron Hedley. Undeterred, Hedley returned to the game and took three wickets to help his side win and remain top of the league. A 20-year-old man was arrested. (2002)

A **bushfire** raging barely a hundred yards from the middle initially failed to stop play in Cessnock, northern New South Wales. The third-grade match between Kurri Kurri and Cessnock Supporters Club carried on even though homes were being evacuated in the area. Only when the wind changed an hour later did the players finally surrender. (2002)

An **electric buggy** stopped play during a match between West Blatchington and St Matthias in East Sussex, when a spectator parked himself on the extra-cover boundary. Taking exception when one of the fielders requested that he move the vehicle, the driver allegedly tried to run down the cricketers, then parked on the pitch and steadfastly refused to budge. Only after a plea from a relative did the invader depart and play resume. (2004)

Henry, a **golden labrador**, held up play for seven minutes in the match between Nynehead and Wombats in Somerset by fielding the ball with his mouth and refusing to drop it. (2004)

A **car crash** outside the ground stopped play in the match between Rusthall and Chelsfield Park. Each side happened to be fielding a doctor, and they rushed off to help the injured. (2005)

An air ambulance **helicopter** (1) stopped play in the match between Babington and Ditcheat, played in the grounds of the Babington House hotel, Somerset. It landed to take an injured chef to hospital. (2005)

A **block of ice** stopped play when it fell from a clear sky on a warm afternoon at Davington Priory, Kent. A Murston batsman was taken to hospital after collapsing, and the ice – about ten feet square – only just missed an umpire. Priory captain Graham Owen said the ice exploded on the pitch. "There was an enormous 'whoosh', and then slush just spread across the ground. We looked around in amazement, but couldn't see any aircraft or anything else it could have come from." (2005)

A **bull** (1) stopped play in the Second Eleven Championship match between Derbyshire and Leicestershire at Dunstall. Derbyshire coach Karl Krikken thought the bull had been frustrated in a failed romantic episode. "It jumped the fence and ran on to the ground, chasing players and spectators for twenty minutes." (2005)

In Bedfordshire, a **flying sightscreen** stopped play when it was caught by a gust of wind and hurtled towards the River Ouse while Olney Town and Willen Second Elevens were playing. The players recaptured it just short of the water. The game resumed after the screen was tethered to a tree. (2005)

Play was stopped in mid-over during the Hampshire Hogs v Hottentots match at Warnford after fielders objected to a batsman's "unnecessarily stentorian" **calling**. (2006)

Students playing at the Shalika Grounds, Colombo, narrowly escaped harm when a **helicopter** (2) landed on the outfield. Junior government minister Mervyn Silva appeared, boarded the helicopter and flew off. (2008)

Play in a one-day match between Himachal Pradesh and Punjab at Una was halted when a **helicopter** (3) landed on the field by mistake. The pilot thought the H for Himachal painted on the pitch was a landing pad. (2009)

The league match in Essex between Frinton and Abberton was abandoned after two Abberton **fielders collided**. Matt Gilray and Mark Copson were both taken to hospital. Umpire Martin White said neither team wanted to continue: "Gilray was in a bad way and Copson didn't know what time of day it was." (2009)

The second day of a Sri Lankan school match between St Sylvester's College and Kalutara Vidyalaya in Kandy had to be abandoned after an air force **helicopter** (4) carrying a politician landed on the ground before the start and remained there all day. Players waited in vain for the return of Faizer Mustapha, former minister for tourism promotion. (2010)

A **white tiger** stopped play for 20 minutes between Hampshire Academy and South Wiltshire at the Rose Bowl, Southampton. The police had received a call alerting them to the beast's presence in a nearby field. Officers went to the scene and, said a spokesman, "they confirmed they were looking at it and it was looking at them". The cricketers and golfers on a nearby course were told to go indoors; a helicopter was scrambled; a team from Marwell Zoo was put on standby with tranquilliser darts; and contingency plans were made to close the M27. It was only when police on the ground noticed the tiger was not moving, and the helicopter team said its thermal imaging cameras could not find a heat source, that officers realised that they were indeed confronted with a tiger. A stuffed toy one. (2011)

The Lake District villages of Threlkeld and Braithwaite, who specialise in finding strange places to play cricket matches, chose to stage a pre-Christmas fixture in one of the huge underground caverns inside the Honister slate mine. (This followed a 2010 match on the snow-capped summit of Latrigg.) The new venue was thought to be weatherproof: unfortunately, a heavy **snowfall** prevented the players reaching the mine. (2011)

The Melbourne Premier match between Prahran and Richmond at Toorak Park was halted after just nine balls when a fielder became suspicious about the **length of the pitch**. It turned out to be at least two metres too long. Test player Cameron White made 147 – on a re-marked pitch. (2012)

An Under-13 match between Scarborough and Bridlington was halted when a **seagull** stole one of the bails. The Scarborough players were coming out to field when the bird swooped on its prize, which was lying just behind the stumps. Umpire Barry Rudd tried to chase the bird but it flew off. Scarborough coach John Green said: "Our lads must have been traumatised by what they'd seen as we lost the game." (2012)

Cambridgeshire's Minor Counties one-day match against Cumberland had to be moved from March to Wisbech because the March Cricket Club pitch had been devastated by **crows**. Club member Pat Ringham said they had caused more damage than "fifty hooligans let loose with golf clubs". The crows were looking for grubs, which were abnormally plentiful; the spray had failed to work owing to an unusually cold March at March. (2013)

Rickmansworth Cricket Club, founded in 1787, have had their season delayed a month after **badgers** dug up the pitch. There were fears play would be impossible all summer, but an ECB grant helped the club re-lay 1,500 square metres of turf. Chairman Mark Raine said the ground looked "as if somebody has turned up with a mortar and tried to trash it". This damage was also blamed on the cold early spring, preventing the groundsman spraying against leatherjackets, which attract badgers. (2013)

The Second Eleven match between Derbyshire and Lancashire at Belper was abandoned after a **series of explosions** and a fire at the former Thorntons chocolate factory nearby. Police advised players to leave the field because of fears there was asbestos in the smoke. (2013)

A Division Six match in the Pembrokeshire County League was abandoned after the batsmen began talking to each other in **Welsh**.

Lamphey Second Eleven player and club chairman Andrew Skeels objected to the language being used by Crymych batsmen Rhydian Wyn and Dyfed Sion, who then walked off. "Thought the days of being told not to speak Welsh in a public place had gone," Sion tweeted. (2013)

Police enquiries stopped play in the Northern League match between Chorley and St Annes, after the visitors discovered that about £1,000 in cash had been stolen from their dressing-room. Police were told an elderly man using a zimmer frame had asked to use the toilets in the dressing-room block rather than hobble across the ground. "It would appear that this old man was not as feeble as he made out," said a police spokesman. St Annes had some compensation: a three-wicket win. (2013)

A **model aircraft** stopped play when it crashed into the square-leg umpire. He was hit on the back of the legs in the match in Leicestershire between Cosby Seconds and Gilmorton. Batsman Nigel Meredith said: "It was just as well the plane hit the ground and bounced before it hit the umpire, otherwise it could really have hurt him. He feigned a bit of injury at first, but then assured everyone he was fine." (2014)

Cycling stopped play when many leagues in Yorkshire rescheduled their fixtures because the 2014 Tour de France started in the county. However, the Darlington & District League carried on, and Dales Cricket Club, based in the Yorkshire village of Reeth, had to put out an SOS asking for "players of any ability" to fulfil an away fixture at Barningham. Their village was in lockdown while the Tour passed through, and ten of their players were unable to drive in or out of their homes. Dales asked the Darlington & District League for the game to be rescheduled but were refused "because it would set a precedent". (2014) *What happened next appears to have gone unreported. Barningham eventually called the game off, saying the ground was unfit. "Were they doing you a favour?"* Wisden *asked Dales secretary Pete McKay. "No, they were not," he said emphatically. "Some really good players had offered to turn out for us, including an ex-county pro who had come up with his family. They wanted to watch the Tour and he didn't. We looked like getting a full team for once."*

Yorkley Star Cricket Club, on the edge of the Forest of Dean in Gloucestershire, is to close after more than 130 years because the pitch, at Cut and Fry Green, is being destroyed by **wild boar**. In 2014, Yorkley were top of their league until the ground was churned up by the boar and their season had to be abandoned. The club paid for the ground to be relaid, but the beasts struck again. Trustee Alec Kear, 80, said: "The forest is overrun with these things. The ground is like a war zone. It's unbelievable. Nothing has stopped play before. We were going all the way through the war, but we just can't cope with this." (2015)

An **angry cabbie** stopped play in the match between Macgregor and Griffith University in Brisbane. A six smashed the cab's windscreen, and the driver avenged himself by driving on to the middle of the pitch. Police persuaded him to move after eight overs had been lost. (2015)

Play was delayed for twenty minutes in the 29th Cricket on Ice tournament in St Moritz because one of the competing teams had forgotten to bring the **nails** needed to secure the matting to the ice. (2016)

A **barn owl** stopped play when it landed on the stumps in the match between Castle Eden and Seaham Park in County Durham. The owl was a pet called Shadow who had squeezed out through the bars of an aviary. Shadow was reunited with his owner, Steven Franklin, after pictures of him started appearing on Facebook. "He's really tame and he wouldn't know how to catch food for himself in the wild," Franklin said. (2016)

All club matches in New South Wales during the second weekend of February were cancelled due to **extreme heat**, with temperatures of 40°C (105°F) forecast. The Sheffield Shield match at the SCG was allowed to go ahead, but officials said they did not have the resources to monitor player safety elsewhere. (2017)

An **irate woman** drove on to the outfield and stopped play in the match between Dales Cricket Club and Luctonians in Leominster, Herefordshire. Unable to find another parking place near her house, she stopped the car, locked it and walked away. Dales asked people to bring their cars into the ground to free up space and the woman came back fifteen minutes later to remove the obstruction. "We are going to send a letter encouraging people to park inside the ground as we do want to be good neighbours," said Dales captain Jon Jones. (2017)

An escaped **bull** (2) stopped play at Kerridge Cricket Club, Cheshire, by racing on to the field and charging after two fielders and an umpire in a match against Mossley. "At first I just thought 'Hello, what's this?' as it was just plodding around the pitch," said Mossley captain Adam Banks. "But then it took one look at me and started charging." Some people took refuge in the nearby pub before the bull wandered off and was recaptured. (2017)

The Kanga Cricket League matches in Mumbai on July 9 were cancelled due to **absence of rain**. "Most of the grounds are underprepared," said the league secretary. (2017) *The Kanga League in Mumbai, named after Dr H.D. Kanga, is a long-established adult league which plays in the*

monsoon season, and is not to be confused with the soft-ball Kanga cricket played by Australian children.

Club fixture lists in Cape Town and across the Western Cape have been slashed for the second season running due to a long-running **drought** and resulting water restrictions. The most senior leagues have been left untouched but in most lower divisions the number of games has been halved. This follows the cancellation of five hundred matches in 2016–17. "Together, we as an urban family must rise to the challenge during a critical juncture of the city's existence," said Western Province Cricket Association president Beresford Williams. (2017)

Seagulls prevented play on the opening day of Somerset's Second Eleven match against Essex at Taunton Vale. They pecked holes in the groundsheets and left the pitch waterlogged. "Once there is a hole in the covers they rip very easily," said Somerset groundsman Rob Hake. "We have just had to spend £12,000 on new covers at our main county ground because they had been damaged by seagulls." (2017)

Judges stopped play after 13 overs in the Under-23 match between Jammu & Kashmir and Goa in Srinagar. The regional high court issued an order halting the game after Hashim Saleem, a J&K player dropped from the squad, lodged a petition claiming that one of the selectors had unjustly picked his own son instead. The match was rescheduled after the court modified the order. (2017)

... AND WHAT DIDN'T

Disaster was narrowly averted when a **pilot** trying to make an emergency landing at Solapur Airport, Maharashtra, suddenly noticed more than five hundred people playing cricket matches on the runway. The Air Deccan aircraft, carrying oil workers, had developed a technical fault and flew over the landing strip twice as a warning. "In the third approach, I landed the aircraft, but to save the people I put on the emergency brakes," said pilot Thomas Lynn. "The craft began skidding at full speed and it stopped when both the rear tyres burst." Bhima Kola, resident of a nearby slum, said they regularly played on the airstrip, and had ignored the plane because there were no regular landings there. (2006)

Northamptonshire and Huntingdonshire's Over-50s teams played on even though the ground at Barnack had been trampled the previous day when a **prize bull and twenty-eight heifers** escaped on to the field. "There were divots and huge holes all over the wickets," said one player. "There were also large deposits of cow dung." (2007)

A swarm of **locusts** failed to stop play in a junior match at Mukinbudin, in the Western Australian wheatbelt. "The oval was covered, and if a ball got hit out to the boundary it would stir them up and they would fly up, and hit the cricketers," said local farmer Jill Squire. "We told the boys to keep their mouths closed." (2013)

The pitch for the Premier League match in Melbourne between St Kilda and Footscray-Edgewater was eight feet **too long**, a fact only discovered after the match, although several players had been puzzled. "Things make sense now," said St Kilda coach Glenn Lalor. "I thought we bowled too short and I think we bowled 27 wides." The job of preparing the ground at Harry Trott Oval is outsourced to a "curation company", which apologised for what it called "an embarrassing situation". (2016)

Pranav Dhanawade, who made the first recorded four-figure individual score in history earlier in the year, was allegedly involved in a brawl with police in Mumbai after trying to prevent a ground where he was playing being used by a **helicopter** (5) for the visit of a government minister. Dhanawade was taken to the police station and given a warning. Meanwhile, the minister, Prakash Javadekar, having heard of the incident, decided to travel by car instead. "It is not proper for me to use the playgrounds as helipad," he said. (2016)

Lymington and Bashley played their Hampshire League Division Three South game bowling only from one end after **vandals** had dug holes in the pitch. "Thankfully, the Bashley captain said they wanted to play and we weren't going to let these hooligans stand in our way," said Lymington captain Chris Tollerfield. (2017)

WHEREVER, WHENEVER

The Earl's Croome club near Worcester have been allowed to use a disused eighteenth-century stately home, Croome Court, as their new headquarters. They play on the back lawn and serve teas in the ninety-foot-long Pink Gallery, designed by Robert Adam. John Rudge, a partner in the development firm that has bought the house, said: "We love the fact that a classic English scene takes place there." (1998)

The Old Alcovians, a team of Northampton businessmen, have found it almost impossible to arrange away fixtures. All their opponents want to play at their new home ground: Earl Compton's ancestral home, Castle Ashby. They were allowed to move there after both the Castle Ashby club and the team from the local village, Yardley Hastings, disbanded. (1998)

Shetland staged its own one-day international when the Cutty Sark Tall Ships race visited. Unfortunately, many boats failed to arrive due to gales, and the only fixture possible was Russia v Germany. No one in either team had ever played before, and the only English speaker was one of the Russians. However, after an hour's coaching a 25-over match was played, which ended in a tie. Only the wicketkeepers wore protective clothing, and the chucking got out of hand – but both teams enjoyed themselves immensely. (1999)

Mudassar Sultan from Lahore, who was leading twenty-two Pakistani pilgrims on the hajj to Mecca, carried a cricket bat aloft as identification to help the group stay together. "There are so many flags here and bamboo sticks with slippers or other objects tied on that I was searching for something unusual," he said. "Not surprisingly, pilgrims notice the bat and can often point out our direction." (2003)

The Hizbul, a militant anti-government group in Kashmir, played a friendly against the Indian Army in the normally tense border area of Kupwara. A large crowd saw the Hizbul beat the Army by 25 runs. However, their commander left immediately the game was over for fear of being arrested by the soldiers. (2000)

An American company that failed to get the rights for India's neutral-venue international matches has bought a cricket ground on the moon in protest. Dreamcricket.com paid $25 to the Lunar Registry for a patch of moonscape near the crater Manilius. Venu Palaparthi, co-founder of the company, said the Dreamcricket Lunar Cricket Field was the perfect venue for Indian cricketers as the low gravity would enable out-of-form batsmen to recover their touch. The legal standing of the purchase is dubious. (2007)

A team of Indian Navy officers on an expedition to the North Pole beat a British team by one run in temperatures of minus 40 degrees. The game was played with strapped-up socks as a ball, ski poles for stumps and a shovel as a bat. (2008)

Members of Sefton Park Cricket Club, Liverpool, played a 20-over match starting at 4.43am (sunrise on the longest day of the year) and finishing in time for the players to go to work. The Long Shadows beat the Early Risers by nine runs, but Chris Brereton failed in his bid to score a fifty before breakfast. The club hope to make the Solstice Cup an annual event. (2010) *The fixture remained in the calendar in 2018 when the Long Shadows, after seven successive defeats, won by one wicket with a ball to spare.*

After four years, cricket returned to Skate Bank, the sand-spit in the Moray Firth which appears only every few years during exceptionally low tides. The previous match in 2006 led to a helicopter and lifeboat being scrambled after a walker thought the players were drowning. This time the players, from Chanonry Sailing Club, warned the coastguard in advance. Crew from eight boats stayed for about half an hour before the waters closed in, and also took part in "extreme ironing", which involves ironing clothes in improbable places. (2010)

The crew of West Mersea lifeboat station in Essex beat their counterparts from Burnham by 13 runs (35 v 22) on an exposed sandbank in the North Sea, five miles off the coast. The match concluded before the tide rose over the bank, despite being held up for several minutes when a dog stole the only ball. (2011)

The Afghan National Army beat a British military team to win a two-day tournament in war-torn Helmand Province. The British also lost to a team of Afghan interpreters. Lt-Col Tim Law of the Royal Artillery said the Afghan side turned out to be "absolutely fantastic". More than 1,500 supporters ran on to the pitch after the soldiers dismissed the British for 75, a 90-run win. (2012)

With the weather so wet that play was obviously impossible, Bournemouth and Oxford decided to settle their British Universities & Colleges quarter-final without either side travelling. The tie was decided by a long-distance bowl-out, staged in their own home-town indoor schools, and watched by umpires who kept in contact by mobile phone. Bournemouth won. (2012)

Lifeboats had to rescue eleven people and a dog after the annual Brambles cricket match in the middle of the Solent. The sandbar pitch, normally exposed for about an hour at the lowest tides of the year, remained water-logged because of a strong westerly wind, and the match had to take place with the players, from two rival yacht clubs, at least ankle-deep in the sea. One boat ran aground, and another had engine trouble on the return journey. (2012)

The United States' two most famous universities, Harvard and Yale, met for their first-ever cricket match, under floodlights in front of a crowd of fifteen. Although Harvard had a team in the nineteenth century, Yale did not, and Harvard cricket had been moribund for more than eighty years. Harvard won by 177 runs. (2012)

In Lancashire, Brooksbottom won their fiftieth anniversary Boxing Day match against Tottington St John's by nine wickets. Alan Fletcher, who started the fixture in 1963, bowled the ceremonial first ball. "We were really lucky with the weather," said Tottington official Kieran Coe. "It stayed dry and mild until we had finished playing, then it poured down."(2012)

The Afghan National Army beat a British Army team by five wickets at Camp Shorabak, the Afghan HQ next to Cape Bastion in Helmand Province. "The Afghans were helped by some wicked deflections to score fours, with the ball hitting loose rocks and evading our fielders," according to British opening batsman Major Kempley Buchan-Smith. (2013)

Threlkeld Cricket Club in Cumberland, whose ground was wrecked by floods in 2012, decided to raise some of the £60,000 needed for repairs by posing for a calendar. However, the players opted out of the now-standard naked pictures ("Most of us are not particularly blessed when it comes to physiques," said treasurer Michael Webster) and instead posed playing cricket in improbable and extreme Lake District locations, ranging from the bottom of Derwentwater to the summit of Latrigg, on Boxing Day. (2013)

The extreme cricketers of Threlkeld Cricket Club added to their collection of crazy venues when they played a match inside the Honister slate mine under Fleetwith Pike, near Buttermere. Using spotlights, a plastic pitch, slate bails – and playing for a slate trophy – Threlkeld lost a six-over match against Caldbeck, who mastered the technique of not getting caught off the wall, instead pushing the ball down the tunnel into the gloom. Threlkeld are hoping they will get their reward by returning to their flood-damaged ground in 2014. A similar match planned a year earlier (*see page 193*) was snowed off when the players could not reach the mine. (2013)

Five players from a London-based nomadic club, The Weekenders, crossed the Channel, armed with donated kit and a length of coconut matting, to play a team of Afghan refugees at the migrant encampment in Calais. Fortified by four extra players picked up in the breakfast queue on the ferry, and two more donated by the Afghans, they managed to play an 11-a-side Twenty20 match. "The odd thing was that once the game started it felt like any other weekend friendly," wrote Weekenders secretary Christopher Douglas. "The unusual local conditions, such as the menacing presence of the riot police truck glimpsed through the trees and an earth-shaking sound system rigged up by the Eritreans, seemed no more threatening than an overhanging Buckinghamshire beech bough. We simply became absorbed in the game." (2015)

WINNERS AND LOSERS

An Essex woman won £62,623 by betting £159,000 that the Lord's Test would end in a draw. Bookmakers William Hill refused to name her, but a spokesman said: "She'd be the one in the middle of the road pointing towards Lord's and doing a rain dance." (1997)

The former England captain Mike Atherton netted a one-sixth share of £68,000 after his syndicate won the Tote Scoop6 horse-racing jackpot. Atherton was commentating on the Trent Bridge Test for Channel 4 when Certain Justice won the 2.45 at Newmarket; his colleague Richie Benaud cheered the mount home for him. (2002)

Ho Sen Hing, a Mumbai resident of Chinese origin, hanged himself after losing a large sum betting on India to beat Bangladesh at the World Cup. (2007)

The vegan teetotaller Greg Chappell has fulfilled two-thirds of a promise to his very unvegan and unteetotal old team-mate Doug Walters. Chappell had said he would eat a steak, drink beer and smoke a cigarette if Walters managed to live until his sixtieth birthday – and he reached the milestone in 2005. "Yep, he honoured the bet," said Walters. "He didn't go with the smoking part, but he had the steak and he had the beers. I think he enjoyed it. I'm sure it did him the world of good." (2007) *and then…*

After forty-three years and an estimated 785,300 cigarettes, former Australian batting hero Doug Walters, 64, says he has given up smoking after undergoing laser treatment in a Sydney clinic. Walters, a former seventy to eighty-a-day man, said he would continue to drink beer and bet. (2010)

The German footballer Didi Hamann claimed to have lost £288,400 on a single cricket spread bet. In his autobiography, Hamann – best-remembered as a defensive midfielder with Liverpool – said he had "bought" an Australian innings against South Africa at 340 for £2,800 a run. Australia collapsed for 237, thus costing him 103 x £2,800. "The next day, when I looked at the mess that was me in the mirror, I said, 'Didi, things have got to change.'" (2012)

At least nine diamond traders in the Indian gem-dealing centre of Surat have defaulted on payments in the past ten days, apparently after losing large sums betting on the IPL. Officials of the Surat Diamond Association said such incidents have become regular occurrences after the conclusion of each IPL season. (2014)

Angela Reakes, who plays for the ACT Meteors in the Australian Women's League, has been given a two-year suspended ban for placing five bets, totalling nine dollars, on the match award for the men's World Cup final. The chief of Cricket Australia's integrity unit said: "All elite cricketers are reminded regularly that betting on any form of cricket is strictly prohibited." (2015)

Police in Kanpur are looking for a man alleged to have lost his wife having used her as his stake when betting on an IPL match. He was said to have run through all his money in previous bets. (2016)

PREQUEL: FROM THE *SPORTSPAGES ALMANAC*

1989

Fred Trueman organised a dinner in London which raised £70,000 for his former new-ball partner Brian Statham, who was suffering from the bone disease osteoporosis.

England captain David Gower revealed that he had been rejected as a playing member of MCC because he could not play the requisite number of qualifying matches and was on the ordinary thirty-year waiting list.

Stuart Welch, 18, a member of the MCC groundstaff, won the search-for-a-spinner competition at Lord's. First prize: a place on the MCC groundstaff.

Also at Lord's, MCC appointed a female PR adviser, Karen Earl; 70% of MCC members who answered a club questionnaire were against admitting women to the club; Sheila Nicholls, 19, did a naked cartwheel in front of the Warner Stand during a one-day international.

Oxfordshire became Minor Counties champions, beating Hertfordshire in the final. Hertfordshire had won the East division title when Andy Needham bowled six successive deliberate and gentle no-balls at Northumberland batsman Peter Graham. The aim was to keep the batsmen interested in victory and stop them playing for a draw. It worked.

Two slow left-armers, Paul Meehan, 51, and Matt Holland, 17, bowled together for Wiltshire against Wales.

Stockport and Littleborough both thought they had won the Central Lancashire League owing to a mix-up over Stockport's points; Littleborough were unlucky.

Hambledon, the best club in England in the eighteenth century, reached the final of the national village competition only to lose to a less evocative team from Cheshire called Toft, who promptly had the trophy stolen.

A fund-raising match at Twyford, Bristol brought in £44; unfortunately the club had to pay £45 to repair a window broken by a six.

In Surrey, a bowler called Malik of Limpsfield Chart took all eleven Chaldon wickets – the teams each had an extra man and agreed to play twelve-a-side.

In Gloucestershire, Dave Debidin of Old Emanuel bowled an over to Ian Payne of Wingate in which the ball did not touch the playing surface: six full tosses were all hit for six.

A ball hit into an adjoining field at Kentisbeare, Devon, was eaten by a cow.

John Overy, umpiring Wimbledon v Stanmore, walked off the pitch with ten overs to go, claiming that several Wimbledon players were drunk.

Two Pembrokeshire teams, Burton and Lawrenny, playing each other in the 22-over Alex Colley Cup, tied three successive matches before Burton won the fourth game by nine wickets. The second tie was caused by the non-striker thinking the ball had gone for four and omitting to run.

George Smith, 44, of Coventry lay down on the wicket for fifteen minutes at the Coventry & North Warwickshire ground to protest against the ball being hit through his sitting-room window.

A game between Burridge in Hampshire and a team from Yorkshire was reportedly interrupted continually by the Burridge players' portable telephones; several misfields were attributed to fielders taking calls. *The word "mobile" was not yet in common use.*

Prajapati All-Indian Club in the West Riding Sunday Cricket Council registered forty-three players for the season – thirty-nine of them called Mistry, thus outdoing by some way the Indian Panthers, who had sixteen Singhs.

Christopher Thomason, 16, made 265 with 20 sixes in a 32-over match for Richard Taunton College in Southampton against Hill College, and then took four wickets for six.

Zac Morris, 10, took five wickets in his first over for Barnsley Under-11s against Derby and was then banned from bowling by teachers in the interests of fairness. Derby won.

Sachin Tendulkar, aged 15 years seven months, scored 100 on debut in the Ranji Trophy for Bombay against Gujarat.

Two former Indian Test players, Jasu Patel and R. H. Shodhan, went on hunger strike until the deputy mayor of Ahmedabad agreed to consider their plea that important matches should be staged at the city's reno-vated Sardar Patel Stadium.

In Pakistan, Haroon Rashid resigned from the selection panel after escaping a gunshot attack on him in Karachi. It is believed the attackers were supporters of players overlooked for the Under-19 squad.

Mike Gatting's least favourite umpire, Shakoor Rana, was dropped from the Pakistani Test panel for refusing to undergo a refresher course.

A man who beat an umpire unconscious with a bat in Winnipeg, Canada, was acquitted of attempted murder but found guilty of aggravated assault and possession of a dangerous weapon.

It was claimed, in a letter to *The Times*, that a competitive cricket league was operating among the native women of the French Pacific island of New Caledonia, with men traditionally doing only the scoring. It was suggested that they would be worthy opponents for England, who were being heavily beaten in the 1989 Ashes.

1990

The last-but-one major ground to deny women access to the pavilion relented in the spring when Lancashire voted to offer them full membership. It transpired that one woman was already in: Ms Stephanie Lloyd rose at the AGM to announce that she had joined the club before her operation when she was Mr K. Hull.

The last male bastion, Lord's, remained impregnable. Mrs Pat Lloyd (no relation to Stephanie), a Glamorgan committee member, was barred from the pavilion during her team's NatWest quarter-final there. "I wasn't going to stand in my suspenders, knock on the pavilion door and demand to get in," she said. The former England women's captain Rachael Heyhoe Flint applied to join, having discovered that no rule specifically forbade women from becoming members. Colonel John Stephenson, the MCC secretary, speculated that women would be allowed in the pavilion, perhaps in the twenty-second century. *The club finally voted to admit female members in 1998.*

Two hundred seats from the Lord's pavilion were offered to MCC members and all were snapped up in a week. "There's been a greater clamour for these seats than for Test match tickets," said a spokesman. "It's been total chaos."

The Indoor Cricket Federation said it was worried by obscenities and taunting of players at their knockout cup. "We didn't get fights or anything like that," said the ICF chairman Peter Robinson, "but I don't even like to see people stubbing out cigarettes on the carpet."

The game between France and Germany in the European Cricketer Cup in Guernsey came close to fisticuffs when a German bowler, Francis Stewart (actually Australian) threw the ball in celebration at a dismissed French batsman Nigel Drummond (actually English) and hit him on the legs. Drummond threw his bat at the bowler. "These are the Friendly Games," said Mike Burbridge of the Guernsey Tourist Board.

In Bhopal, India, during the Nehru Cup, a boy killed his brother for predicting that Pakistan would win the competition. They did.

The Gloucester helmet-makers, WG Cricket, reported a 1,000% rise in sales.

Edgar Watts of Bungay, once Bradman's bat-makers, announced the firm was closing because gales had led to a shortage of mature willows.

Callers ringing a TV phone-in on the future of Yorkshire cricket instead found themselves put through to a helpline on the problems of premature ejaculation. British Telecom said it was their engineers' fault.

Cyril Hollinshead, an 88-year-old slow left-armer, took three wickets in five overs in a game in Gloucestershire.

Dennis Bishop, a 77-year-old off-spinner who plays for the Stanford-le-Hope club in Essex, took his 5,000th wicket since he began keeping records after the war; he first played in 1928 but did not bother counting then.

Harold Stead, 69, who had played for Boconnoc in Cornwall since he was nine, left the club to play for its rivals Penharrow.

Jack Green, 68, headed the winning four for the Co-op in Sheffield against Eastwoods.

Sam Bardney, 15, asked to make up the numbers for Warmsworth in Doncaster, took all ten wickets against Brecks.

In Essex, Simon Harrington, playing for Halstead against Hadleigh, took a hat-trick comprising three members of the same family: Steve Claireaux, his brother Vincent, and his father Clive.

Alton Second Eleven were bowled out by Bournemouth for nought. "It was just one of those days," said their captain Steve Goater.

In County Durham, Darlington beat Billingham Synthonia without a run coming off the bat. Only two Synthonia players turned up and one, Steven Eland, was bowled fourth ball for nought. He then bowled a wide when Darlington's openers batted with their team-mates acting as fielders.

PC Steve Crouch, playing for Sudbury Police against Newton Green, had the apposite bowling figures of nine for nine in nine overs.

Edward Palmer, 15, playing in a junior colts' match for Winchester against Canford, scored 103 and took ten for 13.

Bill Kingston of St Michaels bowled Peter Teckman of the Bold Dragoon at 4.17am on June 21, at the start of a Longest Day charity match in Northampton.

Andrew Mathewman of Penistone, Yorkshire, left a game to take his wife to hospital where she gave birth to a daughter. He returned to run out the last batsman.

A shower of wheat stalks stopped play at Devizes, though there was no wind and no fields nearby.

Roger and Tracey Weston of Worcester named their baby son Liam Bobby so he could have the initials LBW.

Dr Donald Curran, writing in the *Australian Medical Journal*, said the tradition of Australian players drinking their way from Sydney to London before a tour could prove lethal. David Boon was said to have drunk fifty-eight cans of beer en route to the 1989 tour of England, breaking Rod Marsh's record of fifty; Boon, however, was helped by a longer stopover in Bahrain.

The Association of Cricket Statisticians revealed that Sir Donald Bradman attended 1,713 committee meetings of the South Australian Cricket Association between September 1935 and June 1986.

Lynette Batt met Jeremy Ball at an indoor school in Perth and subsequently married him.

The phrase "le cricket" was accepted by the Academie Française as part of the French language, along with "le cowboy" and "la cover-girl".

1991

MCC voted to formalise their unofficial ban on female members after Rachael Heyhoe Flint's application to join the previous year. An attempt to allow honorary women members gained a majority but not a sufficient one. Mrs Flint said women should boycott pavilion tea-making duties in protest.

Wrekin College's girls team, captained by Claire Taylor (daughter of Bob of Derbyshire and England), beat Ellesmere College, captained by Melissa Lloyd (daughter of Clive of Lancashire and West Indies).

Jacqui Hawker, 10, was made captain of Plympton Under-11s to the disgust of her team-mates: "We are not going to be told how to play by a girl," said one boy. "They'll soon see I'm not to be messed with," said Jacqui.

A survey in schools in Kent and south-east London, a traditional hotbed of cricket, showed that 167 teams and 1,680 fixtures had vanished in the past ten years. In north London, Willesden High School, which produced two 1991 England players, Phil DeFreitas and Chris Lewis, was said to be playing only Gaelic football.

Detective-Constable Brian Arkle, playing for Gateshead Fell against Durham City, arrested a dressing-room thief, then went out and scored his maiden century.

Vaughn Walsh, a 26-year-old plumber from Antigua who was rumoured to be the world's fastest bowler, took nine for two, including four wickets in successive balls for his club Leicester Nomads. The last man refused to bat against him. Walsh was offered a game for Somerset against the Sri Lankans but dropped out at the last minute.

Bill Nimmo took all ten wickets for 20 for Scalebor Park against Leeds Police without the aid of a fielder: eight were bowled, two went to return catches.

Malcolm Eustace, captain of Moseley in the Birmingham League, declared at 16 for nine against Old Hill to make the score look better in the record books; Eustace was one of seven players out for a duck.

In the Yorkshire League, Harrogate's captain Austin Jelfs insisted on a prompt start even though eight Cleethorpes players had not yet arrived; Cleethorpes were forced to declare at 11 for two and Harrogate had twelve points deducted for not playing "in the proper spirit of the game". "If I'd been really unsporting," said Jelfs, "I would have batted first."

In Cornwall, Jed Bowers, the wicketkeeper for Trevone, completed a hat-trick with his first delivery of 1991, having taken two wickets with the last two balls of his previous spell – two years earlier.

Near Bath, Ellis Lyppiatt, playing for South Stoke against Priston, needed to hit a four to win but had his shot blocked by a duck waddling across the edge of the outfield.

Terry Sutherland, 52, batting at Dunston, Norfolk, was struck on the trouser pocket and the ball ignited a box of matches.

Jack Hyams, 71, made what was reported to be his 169th century, playing in an Over-35s match for Cockfosters against Winchmore Hill. *See also page 10.*

Brian Tancock, 66, took eight wickets in the opening game of his fifty-third season for Ashill, Somerset.

The Herald Cricket Club, in Milton Keynes, having finished bottom of its league for three successive seasons, found itself with funds of £70 and a bill for pitch hire of £350. It stuck the entire kitty on a horse called Buddy Holly, which won at Plumpton at 6 to1.

Coldharbour Cricket Club in Surrey hired The Oval for a special match to celebrate 62-year-old Reg Comber's fifty years in the team.

The game near Bath between the Compton Dando village team and the Compton pub was abandoned after the village team captain ejected one of the opposing players from the pavilion. Three years earlier, the victim had named the captain as co-respondent in his divorce suit.

Fred Goodall, the former New Zealand Test umpire, married Di Malthus, a woman he met when she was playing and he gave her out.

Fred Trueman's daughter Rebecca married Raquel Welch's son Damon and had her union blessed at Bolton Abbey, Yorkshire, on the eve of the Headingley Test. Ms Welch upstaged the bride and upset her father by arriving ten minutes late and under-clothed. "I think she left half her dress behind," said Fred. *The marriage was over little more than a year later: "It didn't last as long as my run-up," Trueman observed.*

Cricket returned to Iran for the first time since the Ayatollah-led Revolution twelve years earlier when a five-a-side tournament was held in the British Embassy garden; a ball out of the grounds was deemed to be out rather than six because of a shortage of balls and the need not to upset the Iranians.

The Royal Navy nuclear submarine HMS *Tireless* and the American sub USS *Pargo* broke through the ice in the Antarctic so the crews could play each other; unfortunately, the Americans failed to grasp the Laws and lost by 187 runs to eight homers.